CHINS

(Child in Need of Supervision)

Russ Ambrose

I am making available physical copies of this work at the lowest possible price. In return, you are encouraged to make a charitable donation if you find value or solace within these pages.

As for the charity to which you hopefully contribute, you should each construct your own adventure, so to speak, and donate to the cause(s) and/or organization(s) you consider appropriate in light of any value you receive from this work. However, if you are unable to select an appropriate cause or organization to which to donate, perhaps consider the following suggestions:

Helen DeVos Children's Hospital Child Psychiatry Clinic

Mary Free Bed Rehabilitation Hospital – Association for the Blind and Visually Impaired

To the countless people on whose
shoulders I stand

FOREWARD

We all have the capacity to help others heal, a gift which is enhanced by our own good health. Thus, one of the best things we can do for this world is to work on healing ourselves. So many people I see come in feeling hopeless and lost and defeated because they think this is the life they're stuck with. They've tried to fix things on their own and haven't been successful. But in reality, the brain retains its plasticity even as we age. Rapid, drastic, and lasting change is possible, as long as you are open to it, it can just be hard to imagine. It's hard work to try instead of just staying how you are. But to say you don't need help or therapy is to say that things are fine just the way they are, and that's usually not the case. There's always room for improvement or a fresh perspective. This work offers knowledge, insight, and even laughter. But most of all, it should give you hope. That change and healing is much more possible than you realize. That you're not the only one trying. That if another person can do it, you can do it too. You just have to be willing to start somewhere. It's never too late to start being the person you want to be.

Kathryn Barcelona, LMSW

INTRODUCTION

They say everyone has a book in them,
but no one ever tells you how hard it is
to get that book out of you.

Chantel Prat, Ph.D., *The Neuroscience of
You*

There exists a widely viewed video in which
Matthew McConnaughey is speaking to a group of
students about "life lessons." Predictably,
McConnaughey informed his audience that "life is
not easy" and "life is not fair" and, therefore, you
should "not fall into the trap. . .of feeling like you're
a victim." Instead, McConnaughey instructed his
audience to just "get over it and get on with it."

Hard to take issue, in a general sense, with this
sentiment, but agreeing with the sentiment and
understanding how to accomplish it are two very
different things. Many of life's obstacles can
undoubtedly be overcome through some combination
of effort and force of will as McConnaughey suggests.
However, what about when hard work and
determination are insufficient, not due to any
personal failings but rather because your own body,
at a sub-conscious level, is actively working against
you in ways you are unable to identify or
understand? This is the landscape that trauma
leaves in its wake.

As I navigated my mid-to-late 50s, this did not seem like a topic that should occupy my time or energy. My life appeared to be in a relatively good place both personally and professionally. However, while I certainly had a great deal in life to be thankful for, I nevertheless continued to feel overwhelmed by the destructive thoughts and images which far too often intruded into my waking (and sleeping) hours. The genesis of my distress concerned matters I neither wanted to openly acknowledge nor confront as it involved painful circumstances which caused my life to unravel until I just hit rock bottom. Then, unable to manage the pain and emotions eating me from the inside out, I just stuffed it all in a box, buried it deep within the recesses of my mind, and just tried to "power through." While this approach was not without its apparent moments of success, peace of mind remained elusive. I doubt this was what McConnaughey had in mind.

Instinctively, I realized that while I had come quite far since bottoming out, the box I had disregarded for so long had to be brought into the open and its contents confronted. As if to underscore the magnitude of this observation, my initial conversation with a therapist went sideways after only a few minutes with me reduced to blubbering semi-coherence. So, the conclusion that I was, at least at some level, an absolute mess was not really news. Nevertheless, learning, several weeks later, that I had been diagnosed with Chronic Post Traumatic Stress Disorder (PTSD) certainly got my attention.

My first thought was that this diagnosis seemed a bit melodramatic. In my mind, PTSD was what combat veterans and survivors of horrific events like mass shootings experience. As I would come to realize, however, while such life and death circumstances can certainly be traumatic, potentially traumatic events are much more ubiquitous and encompass a far greater range of the human experience. Considering the experiences I had for many years failed to directly confront, and the impact my inaction had (and still has) on my physical and emotional health, I was compelled to accept my therapist's assessment.

Sigmund Freud once famously diagnosed a man by declaring, "I think this man is suffering from memories." It seems ironic that the memories and imprints of events which I have worked so hard to forget and disregard could cause so much suffering, but suffer I have. This work is partly an effort to identify some of what I experienced, describe its impact, and illustrate the consequences of failing (or refusing), for far too many years, to acknowledge and confront these events. I also hope to highlight much of the assistance I have received over the years from so many people and describe how it has helped me. In the process I hope to provide something which can help others experiencing similar difficulties or who want to better understand how to help someone else.

I am not a mental health professional and this work is certainly not presented as some sort of how-to guide. Nonetheless, I can confidently state from experience that responding to pain, trauma, and life's general (and inevitable) bullshit by pretending it did not happen and will, therefore, just magically evaporate from your memory and consciousness is unhealthy self-deception. Either you "control" your trauma or it will "control" you, the latter being a circumstance which is unhealthy at best and potentially life threatening at worst. Trauma, unacknowledged and unconfronted, can wreak havoc on your ability to function and poison your view of the world and yourself. Ignoring trauma only magnifies its presence and impact whereas openly acknowledging and confronting it is the only effective way to deprive it of its destructive power.

Despite their role in my story, my experiences are not something I relish discussing. Most of the experiences I describe are things which, prior to undertaking this effort, I have shared (if at all) with only one other person. These are things about which I simply don't speak or otherwise acknowledge. I certainly never before considered writing about such things. So, if discussing these topics is so unpleasant, why do this. Why not spend my time doing something more enjoyable like being waterboarded or doing my taxes. The short answer is that I am doing this out of necessity.

We are not (yet) robots and our brains do not function like computer hard drives. Thus, it is not possible to simply erase from our consciousness the memories of traumatic events. Moreover, our brains actually remember and organize memories of traumatic events very differently. This difference is at least partially responsible for many of the struggles experienced by individuals with PTSD. I am learning, however, that it is possible to alter the way that my brain and body interpret and organize certain memories and events so that they become less intrusive and destructive.

In his book *The Body Keeps the Score*, Dr. Bessel Van Der Kolk observes that "[a]fter trauma the world is experienced with a different nervous system that has an altered perception of risk and safety." Trauma not only alters or interferes with an individual's emotional well-being but also produces physical changes which are counterproductive to one's overall well-being. As Dr. Van Der Kolk further observes, "[w]e have learned that trauma is not just an event that took place sometime in the past; it is also the imprint left by that experience on mind, brain, and body. This imprint has ongoing consequences for how the human organism manages to survive in the present. Trauma results in a fundamental reorganization of the way mind and brain manage perceptions."

Accordingly, because trauma results in physical changes to the individual's brain and body, truly effective treatment must go beyond simply treating the individual's emotions or emotional state. To be effective, treatment must also recognize the physical harm visited on the body by trauma (and its aftermath) and incorporate treatment of such. In fact, it is often not possible to effectively treat an individual's emotional state without first inducing a physical change in the way their brain and body interpret, process, and respond to information and stimuli.

Fortunately, I am working with a talented therapist whose treatment approach incorporates this understanding. One of the first things she encouraged me to do was an activity designed to begin modifying the way my brain interprets and interacts with certain memories and events. Specifically, she asked me to begin consciously recognizing when, and under what circumstances, some of my more negative or unhealthy thoughts begin to intrude. Because so many unproductive and unhealthy thought processes occur at a level below conscious thought, the first step to redirecting my negative or unproductive mental energy was to learn to recognize when my subconscious thought processes (i.e., my mental muscle memory) were undermining me.

After attempting this for a short time, I became a bit frustrated at the randomness and passivity of this approach. I'm not getting any younger, so why sit around waiting for the negative thoughts to find me, especially when part of my problem is that I often don't even recognize when my mental muscle memory is undermining me? I've had this bullshit running around in my head for close to 50 years, so it's not like I don't know where to find it. So, why not take this stuff head-on – start writing about the events and experiences causing me so much difficulty and force all this stuff out into the open where it can more easily be confronted. Thus, what began as brief thoughts written for myself quickly transformed into what eventually became this work.

Time will ultimately judge the efficacy of this approach, however, I have already begun to perceive a difference in my internal relationship with the events and experiences in question. I am beginning to experience a quietness of mind with which I am unfamiliar and am beginning to feel some measure of control over things that have, for most of my life, exerted extraordinary control over me. To accomplish this, however, I have had to acknowledge and engage with the events and circumstances described herein. Thus, in a very real sense, I *had* to write to book, if only for myself.

While I *wrote* this book for myself, I have chosen to *share* it, in part, because I am confident it can in some way benefit others. It may be easy to conclude that I am sharing this work out of a belief that what I experienced is somehow unique. The reality is quite the opposite. Sadly, I am well aware that there is nothing about what I experienced that is unique. It is almost guaranteed that everybody who reads this will relate, in some personal way, to the events and experiences described herein.

Perhaps you will find something in these pages that helps you try to navigate some of life's inevitable bullshit. You may instead know somebody who is struggling with something that they just cannot seem to work through. You may want to help but are just not sure how. While I have worked very hard to arrive at a reasonably good place in life, this was simply not possible without the help of a great many people. Perhaps reading about their efforts will give you some insight and/or motivate you to help somebody else.

Trauma and general bullshit is part of the human experience and impacts all of us, directly or indirectly, more than we likely realize. The advances and insights being made in the treatment of PTSD and related conditions, and the science underlying such, are fascinating. Treatment of PTSD and related impairments is certainly more art than science. Such does not, however, relegate science to the kid's table. To the contrary, significant treatment breakthroughs have been made in recent years thanks to important scientific advancements. For example, advances in medical technology have enabled researchers and care providers to visualize and study the brain in ways never before possible. Dr. Van Der Kolk describes this advancement:

> In the early 1990s novel brain-imaging techniques opened up undreamed-of capacities to gain a sophisticated understanding about the way the brain processes information. . .For the first time we could watch the brain as it processed memories, sensations, and emotions and begin to map the circuits of mind and consciousness. The earlier technology of measuring brain chemicals like serotonin or

norepinephrine had enabled scientists to look at what *fueled* neural activity, which is a bit like trying to understand a car's engine by studying gasoline. Neuroimaging made it possible to see inside the engine. By doing so it has also transformed our understanding of trauma.[1]

---

[1] A full understanding of these advancements and their impact is well beyond the scope of this work (and certainly beyond my nascent understanding). Nevertheless, because such is relevant to this work, I have attempted to incorporate such as much as possible. However, because I make no claims to be a scientist, therapist, or anything remotely resembling an expert, I freely quote from multiple sources. My primary goal is to avoid confusion about the source of certain things I discuss and describe herein. Much of what I have read and learned is reasonably easy to understand and has been incorporated and synthesized with my pre-existing knowledge. I feel reasonably comfortable and competent writing about such matters in "my own voice." Other aspects of what I have learned, however, are so fundamental, so important to understanding what I am trying to describe, and/or so obviously not something I could have independently understood or articulated, that it seems best to simply quote from and/or reference the source.

Perhaps my attempts to explore and/or introduce such will pique your interest in this or similar topics. If nothing else, perhaps you'll simply find some entertainment value in reading about somebody whose life has often resembled an episode of Jerry Springer gone sideways. With that out of the way, let's jump in.

While trauma is practically a universal experience, not everybody experiences PTSD or similar long-lasting emotional scars. While there are numerous reasons why this is the case, one of the reasons is undoubtedly parenting. One of the things which distinguishes those who are reasonably well-adjusted from those who endure lengthy struggles with unpleasant life events concerns parenting or parent-like relationships. If you're fortunate, you received the kind of parenting and nurturing that enables you to respond to trauma and unpleasant events in healthy and productive ways. Far too many people, however, myself included, did not experience this kind of parenting. Thus, parenting, in the broadest and most general sense, is an underlying theme of this work.

While my childhood was filled with many moments of joy and happiness, I also experienced more than enough abuse, neglect, and dysfunction. Simply put, with some notable and intermittent exceptions, the adults in my early life did not teach or exhibit the skills I needed to effectively confront and navigate life's more unpleasant events and circumstances. While many children experience homes with stable and healthy parenting, the constants during my childhood were my mother's poor decision making, her unfitness as a parent, and the utter dysfunction that characterized life with her. It is impossible to sum up in a single incident what it was like to live with my mother. There is one incident, however, that perhaps comes close.

In the summer of 1980, I was 16 years old with a car and a part-time job. With a rebellious itch that needed constant scratching, I took every opportunity to escape home and hang out with my friends. By this point in our relationship, my mother must have realized she had little (if any) control over me. Perhaps understanding that she could not lose battles she did not fight, my mother imposed few rules on me. What few rules she did impose were, in my mind, barely suggestions.

One night that summer, I was supposed to be home by midnight. LOL. Well after midnight, my friends and I decided to call it a night and crash at my place. When we rolled in around 2:00 a.m., I fully expected conflict and at least part of me welcomed the opportunity to mix it up with my mother in front of a couple of my friends. When we entered the house, however, we discovered it was empty. My mother and sister were nowhere to be found.

With nobody around, we just plopped down at the kitchen table and started eating and bullshitting. A short time later, my mother strolled through the back door and I instinctively braced for battle. Far from upset, my mother happily waved at us as she walked to the kitchen closet and grabbed a paper sack into which she tossed a gallon whisky bottle. She then strolled into her bedroom, exiting a short time later with a small handful of clothes which she also tossed in the paper sack. My mother then scooped up the sack and scurried out the door proclaiming, "I'm going camping, be back in a week or so."

No indication where, or with whom, this alleged camping excursion was taking place. Likewise, no indication where my sister was or whether she was also going "camping." This incident, while oddly memorable, was not particularly unusual. At this point of her life, between husbands three and four, my mother often stayed away from home for several days (or longer) at a time to seek out and/or visit boyfriends and potential husbands. Even when she was at home, she was rarely engaged with me or my life in any meaningful way.

Regardless, I was glad to see her go and chase whatever shiny thing currently had captured her attention. By this point, the two of us were barely able to coexist under the same roof. My mother apparently felt similarly because the following year she initiated court proceedings to have me removed from her care thereby relieving herself of any ongoing obligation or responsibility for my care.

The Alabama Family Court system, finding me to be a CHINS (Child in Need of Supervision), granted my mother's request. As the court concluded, I was "ungovernable" and "incorrigible" and, apparently, too much for my mother to manage. Fair enough. I was "ungovernable" and "incorrigible" on a good day, and good days were, by this time, few and far between. Nevertheless, to this day I wonder whether the good people of Alabama didn't bestow the CHINS. designation on the wrong operant of the parent-child equation.

<table>
<tr><td>.e of Alabama
Unified Judicial System
Form JU-6 Rev 2/79</td><td>PETITION</td><td>Case Number
JU 81 348
ID YR Number</td></tr>
</table>

IN THE JUVENILE COURT OF _____ FRANKLIN _____ COUNTY

In the Matter of ____ Russell David Ambrose _____, a child DOB __3/14/64__

Address ____ Regency Plaza Apartments, Russellville, AL 35653 _____

Child's Father ____ James McLean Ambrose ____ Address ____ India ____

Child's Mother ____ Nancy Mason ____ Address ____ Regency Plaza Apartments, R'Ville,Al.

Child's Guardian Or
Physical Custodian : Nancy Mason, natural mother Address ____ Regency Plaza Apartments ____

Guardianship, custody, control and supervision of the child is vested in ____ petitioner ____

Complainant's Name ____ Nancy Mason ____
Complainant's Address or Employment ____ Regency Plaza Apartments, Russellville, AL. 35653

The said child is ☐ Delinquent, ☐ Dependant, ☒ In need of supervision in that

     child is ungovernable and incorrigible.

The said child is also in immediate or threatened danger of physical and/or emotional harm in that

     his behavior is ungovernable and incorrigible.

and he should be removed immediately.

I swear that I am informed and believe and state upon such information, knowledge, and belief, that the above allegations and facts are true.

Date ____ 8/5/81 ____ Signature ____ Nancy Mason ____

SWORN TO AND SUBSCRIBED BEFORE ME THIS DATE ____ 8/5/81 ____

In reality, the CHINS proceedings merely formalized the irreparable (and long-standing) rupture in the relationship between me and my mother. It was a rupture that would never be repaired. After the court relieved my mother of responsibility for my care, it would be many years before we even spoke. We later attempted to reconnect and establish some kind of relationship, but it was simply beyond our ability (or desire). Failing to achieve any measure of forgiveness or even forgetfulness, we drifted apart and as a result it has been roughly 30 years since I last communicated with my mother. Given her poor health, I'm certain she passed away years ago.

So, what did I experience that caused the relationship with my mother to deteriorate to the point where she felt compelled to quite literally wash her hands of me? Just how badly would my life come off the rails in the coming years? How did I manage to get my life back on track? And what lessons are there, if any, to be gleaned from my experiences? The answers to these and other related questions, hopefully, lie within these pages.

You can choose your friends but you
'sho can't choose your family.

Harper Lee

In the early summer of 1963, my mother and father,
both age 19, combined to create the life that would,
nine months later, culminate with my birth.
Consistent with the dominant middle-class values of
the 1960s, my parents married later that summer.
While I have little to no conscious memory of my
early years, I apparently spent a great deal of my
time with my paternal grandparents, McLean and
Viola Ambrose. This is evident from photographs
and stories told to me by my grandparents and
others. Amidst the chaos and instability that would
come to characterize my life, my grandparents were
an oasis of calm in the center of a hurricane of
dysfunction.

Other than the fact that my parents' marriage was
short lived, I know very little of the details. I was
never really interested in the subject and it was not
something that came up in conversation with my
parents or grandparents. Knowing each of my
parents, however, I can say with a great deal of
confidence that their marriage was tumultuous and
mutually unsatisfying. Given their fundamental
incompatibility, the fact that they were even willing
to give marriage a go is a testament to then
prevailing social norms, as well as my grandparents'
undoubted insistence that their grandchild not be
born a bastard.

My parents' marriage was officially terminated shortly after my second birthday. After divorcing my father, my mother and I lived in a small apartment in the upstairs of an old house. The only memory I have from this time, oddly enough, concerns an incident in which I tried making pizza in the wee hours. At that time, a popular grocery product was Chef Boy-Ar-Dee Complete Pizza. In the days before ubiquitous pizza delivery, this magical little box contained everything you needed to make your own pizza: (1) dough mix to which you simply added water; (2) a too small can of sauce; and (3) an even smaller can of white powder suspiciously labeled "cheese."

After my mother's second marriage, we regularly ate these homemade pizzas topped with whatever we had available. These events were still in the future, however. At this particular moment I was a hungry preschooler determined to get my snack on in the early morning hours. Many of the details concerning this adventure have been lost to time, but two things are clear in my memory – I made an incredible mess and my pizza was inedible.[2] In retrospect, this incident seems like a metaphor of sorts for this stretch of life. . .chaotic and generally unsatisfying.

At some point, my mother found work at Michigan Bell where she met Ben Thulin, the man who would soon become her second husband. Ben, who was

---

[2] While the quality of my cooking has since improved dramatically, I still consider food preparation a messy contact sport as my wife will frustratingly acknowledge.

almost 20 years my mother's senior, was a widower with six children, Chip, Mike, Dave, Craig, Clark, and Andy, ranging in age from 9 to 17. So, my mother, ill-equipped to raise even one child, assumed the task of caring for and managing seven boys, the oldest of which was only a few years her junior. In short, my mother assumed a task that would have been incredibly difficult for even the most skilled and patient person. Given my mother's personal struggles and deficiencies as both a person and parent, this endeavor was, unfortunately, doomed to fail.

I was still quite young, having not yet begun kindergarten, when my mother and Ben married. Despite my young age, and the fact that their marriage only lasted roughly 6 years, I have good memories from this period. . .playing baseball at every opportunity. . .climbing through neighborhood barns to play war or hide-and-seek. . .visiting with the neighbor kids to play cards or board games. . .working in the garden and canning vegetables. This was also when I began to develop a voracious appetite for reading pretty much anything I could get my hands on.

Not all the memories were positive, however. Ben and my mother seemed a good match at the outset and even had a daughter together. However, my mother was completely overwhelmed by and, in my opinion, not particularly interested in, the difficult work of raising someone else's children all of whom were likely traumatized and/or suffering over the death of their mother. Thus, I recall life during this period being permeated with a general sense of chaos and disquiet punctuated with much yelling and arguing. Also, while certainly not violent people, Ben and my mother often resorted to corporal punishment which on at least one occasion crossed a line that today would neither be ignored nor tolerated.

Less significant concerns included my mother's "food rules" which have always been a sore spot with me. I've long since forgotten many of these edicts, but two have remained etched in my memory. First, my mother was allowed to eat Raisin Bran cereal while the rest of us had to eat Corn Flakes. Certainly nothing wrong with Corn Flakes, but I would have preferred a choice in the matter. Nevertheless, my mother hoarding the Raisin Bran for herself, while irritating, was arguably a "first-world problem" sort of thing.

The other "food rule" that sticks in my memory, however, should have resulted in criminal charges. My mother was allowed to drink real milk while the rest of us had to drink powdered milk. If you don't know what powdered milk is, think of the most horribly tasting pseudo-milk product that the 1960s could produce, throw in some dirty socks, rotten vegetables, and probably a pinch of DDT for flavor, and then let it ferment underground like kimchi. As bad as this concoction probably sounds, actual powdered milk tasted so much worse.

Joking aside, my mother's "food rules" were, if judged in a vacuum, arguably the sort of things that large families with limited means simply did to get by. Just as with gift giving, however, it is the thought that counts. Here, the thought, at least in my mind, was that my mother consistently put herself before anybody else and was unwilling to make any sacrifice for others including her own family. This attitude manifested itself in many other ways and was something I would never forget and which (at least subconsciously) informed my view of my mother as I grew older.

Looking back, while I have memories of many positive moments with Ben, I cannot claim to have really known him. I was so young and he and my mother were married for such a brief period. However, I have been able to know Ben's sons, my brothers, in the almost 50 years since. To the extent you can know a man through his children, I know that Ben was a good and decent man who loved his family. It is unfortunate that my time with Ben was so brief. Judging by my brothers' character, Ben's influence would have been something from which I would have benefitted greatly. Instead, following my mother's divorce from Ben, I was stuck with my mother as she headed south in search of something which she would find, if at all, only many years later.

Child abuse casts a shadow the length
of a lifetime.

Herbert Ward

Shortly after divorcing Ben, my mother (with me
and my younger sister in tow) headed south to the
outskirts of Memphis where her brother Frank lived.
Frank was in the Navy and stationed at the naval
base in nearby Millington. We lived with Frank, his
wife Mary, and their three foster kids. Their kids,
one boy and two girls, all of whom were a couple
years older than me, immediately welcomed me and
included me in their many hijinks and bad behavior.
In short order, I learned how to shoplift, locate (and
consume) alcohol, and sneak out of the house (and
return many hours later) without getting caught.
We also skipped school regularly to hang out and
roam the neighborhood. In short, Frank and Mary's
kids were rebellious and largely uncontrollable and
I was an eager apprentice.

We only lived with Frank and Mary for one year,
however. At the conclusion of the school year, my
mother moved us to the metropolis of Phil Campbell,
Alabama, to be near her sister Dorothy and her
family. Because living with Dorothy was not an
option, we lived in run-down, bug-infested
apartments for several months before finally moving
into a house. Household bugs are simply part of life
in the deep south, so after we got settled into our own
place my mother contacted one of the local pest

control outfits. Soon thereafter, Harvey Mason from City Pest Control rolled up the driveway.

By this point, my mother very much had her sights set on husband number three and Harvey, it turned out, was available and looking.[3] The two hit it off apparently and a very brief courtship immediately commenced. By this point, I'd had enough of my mother's chaotic and dysfunctional search for love. I don't recall being overtly hostile to Harvey, I just tried to ignore him. It wasn't personal (yet), I just had no interest in participating in my mother's circus-like personal life. However, there was nothing I could do to stop the inevitable and in short order my mother and Harvey married.

In addition to controlling pests, and generally failing to control his wandering eye, Harvey was a horse guy. He owned quite a few horses and competed in horse shows throughout the Southeast. In addition to horses, we had chickens, a couple pigs, and a milk cow. Since animals were more enjoyable to me than most people, this all seemed like a positive development. While I enjoyed the animals, I had no experience with, or real knowledge of, horses. So, Harvey enlisted his horse trainer, James, to teach me how to ride and handle horses. James seemed to be a good choice for the task. He trained Harvey's horses (and Harvey) well enough that Harvey was having great success showing his horses.

---

[3] I would subsequently learn that Harvey was always available and never not looking.

James spent a fair amount of time with me and soon I was competent (and confident) enough to saddle-up "my" horse and ride her around the pasture on my own. While I enjoyed hanging out with the horses and riding around our property, I absolutely hated going to horse shows. I didn't know anybody at these silly events and it was boring sitting around watching other people ride and show their horses. Not to mention that I had little desire to spend my weekends hanging out with my mother, my sister, or Harvey.

Knowing this, and apparently content to leave me in James' care, my mother and Harvey (along with my sister) would regularly travel on the weekends all over the Southeast to attend horse shows. At the outset, this was a pretty good arrangement. I got to stay home and largely do what I wanted while avoiding being bored to tears at horse shows. As I would soon learn, however, this arrangement came at an incredible cost. James, it turned out, was a pedophile, something I would be compelled to suffer for many months.

In the Introduction, I posed the question "how did my life, and my relationship with my mother, get to the point where my mother felt the need to quite literally wash her hands of me?" The answer now presents itself. Being sexually assaulted on a regular basis for a prolonged length of time was bad. Really bad. What was probably worse, however, was believing (and still believing) that my mother (and Harvey) knew or should have known what was happening to me and yet did nothing to help or protect me.

In terms of what caused the irreparable fracture in the relationship with my mother, these events were ground zero. Our relationship to this point, like any relationship with my mother, was occasionally positive with turmoil and conflict, however, never far from the surface. After these events, however, our relationship was incapable of being anything other than toxic and destructive. Never again would I trust my mother and I would simply disregard, if only out of spite, anything she said or expected. Combined with my lack of respect for Harvey, the stage was set for me to surrender to the rebellion coursing through my body. The coming rebellion, however, was not undertaken in service of a noble or even constructive goal. Instead, the coming storm reflected my body's instinctive response to the chaos and cruelty visited upon it.

This is perhaps a good time to briefly explore the body's stress response system. The stress response system performs as its name suggests – it responds to stress and threat, prompting us to take action which our brain believes is necessary for our survival and well-being. The way in which the stress response system functions has been imprinted into our DNA over thousands of years of evolution. And while the stress response system is integral to our survival, its activation can exact a toll. As MaryCatherine McDonald, Ph.D., author of *Unbroken – The Trauma Response is Never Wrong*, explains, "[t]hink of your nervous system as a command center. When the stress response system is activated, certain knobs are turned way up and others are turned way down. Functions that are less important in a moment of threat are turned down so that more energy can be sent to support functions that are more important."

Input from our senses is processed from the bottom up. As Dr. Bruce Perry, author of *What Happened to You?*, observes, "[i]nput from all our senses. . .first comes into our brain in the lower areas. None of our sensory input goes directly to the cortex; everything first connects to lower parts of the brain." The lower portions of our brain are often referred to as our lizard brain because lizards don't really think or plan but rather "mostly live in the moment and react."

When our stress response systems are activated, the portions of our brain responsible for higher level function "are turned way down" whereas our lizard brain gets "turned way up." So, when our stress response system is activated, we are not generally accessing or utilizing our higher-level brain functions (e.g., rational thought) but are instead instinctively reacting like a lizard.

The stress response system has been described as the body's "smoke alarm." Think of how a smoke alarm generally works. A smoke alarm doesn't engage in high-level cognitive assessment but is rather pure lizard brain. If its sensors detect "smoke" it immediately starts screaming that a threat exists and that you need to take immediate action. Likewise, if we face a real or potential threat it is healthy for our stress response system to activate, engage our "lizard brain" (while simultaneously shutting-down the higher-level areas of our brain), and prompt us to take immediate action to protect ourselves. This is healthy, adaptive behavior.

We've all probably experienced, however, situations in which the smoke alarm in our home "malfunctioned," activating in the absence of any real threat of fire. It can be an incredibly irritating and disrupting experience. What if our body's internal smoke alarm becomes overly sensitized and activates in response to events it incorrectly perceives as threats? In *What Happened to You?*, Dr. Perry provides a vivid example.

Mike Roseman was a Korean War combat veteran. Following an unsettling incident while he was out with his girlfriend, Sally, the pair visited Dr. Perry where Mike related the following:

> We were going out last night. Had a nice dinner and we were walking downtown on our way to the movies. And suddenly I was in the street, between parked cars, on my belly with my hands over my head, terrified. I thought we were being shot at. I was pretty confused, I guess. At some point, I realized that a motorcycle had backfired. Sounded like gunfire. The knees on my suit were torn. I was

sweaty, my heart was racing. I was so embarrassed. Felt like I was jumping out of my skin. I just wanted to go home and get drunk.

Sally then added:

One minute we were arm in arm, the next he is back in a foxhole in Korea, screaming. I tried to get down and help him, but he just pushed me away. He hit me. It seems like it lasted for ten minutes, but I think it was only a couple of minutes.

For Mike, behavior that was, in one context, adaptive and healthy had become maladaptive and unhealthy. As Dr. Perry explained to Mike, "[w]hat kept you alive in Korea is killing you back home." This circumstance, where an individual engages in behavior that was once healthy and adaptive but is, in present circumstances unhealthy and maladaptive, is one of the ways in which PTSD manifests. Similarly, as Dr. Van Der Kolk explains, a person experiencing a traumatic event is "never the same again. The trauma may be over, but it keeps being replayed in continually recycling memories and in a reorganized nervous system."

By this point in my brief life, my body's stress response system had received a workout sufficient for several lifetimes. In psychological or neurological terms, my stress response system had become "sensitized" (i.e., hyper-aroused or hypervigilant). In simpler terms, my lizard brain, which perceived threat around every corner, was in control of my behavior to an extent that was neither healthy nor productive.

As Dr. Perry explains, when people whose stress response systems have become sensitized are exposed to "minor stressors," their response oftentimes is to react "as though they were facing great threat." His experience and research working with individuals experiencing this type of sensitization revealed that "[i]n some cases the brain systems associated with the stress response had become so active that they eventually 'burnt out' and lost their ability to regulate the other functions they would normally mediate. As a result the brain's capacity to regulate mood, social interactions, and abstract cognition was also compromised." This is an apt description of what I was then experiencing.

Simply put, I began to experience extreme emotional or neurological dysregulation. The concept of dysregulation covers a lot of territory, however, for present purposes I find Dr. Perry's general articulation of such appropriate – an inability to control or regulate your emotional response to circumstances or to respond in ways viewed as unacceptable or unreasonable. As explored below, I was becoming, unfortunately, the epitome of a dysregulated child.

Thus, my circumstance as I transitioned into my teenage years was not exactly encouraging. I was confused and hurt, unwilling and/or unable to trust the adults in my life and lacking the skills or support structure necessary to navigate the strange and turbulent waters in which I found myself. I felt like a wounded animal, injured in ways I could not understand and unsure what help I needed, if such help even existed, and, if so, where it could be found. As Dr. McDonald puts it, "[t]he traumatic experience has written itself into the body. Trauma has revealed the world to be fundamentally dangerous in a way that biology will not forget." I would articulate it much more viscerally - having experienced life as prey, I experienced the world as a dangerous and unsafe place populated with predators. I responded accordingly, lashing out at pretty much everybody and everything in my path.

Before exploring the various ways in which my dysregulation and dysfunction manifested, there is a difficult question that I cannot (but would prefer to) ignore. A question which has robbed me of much sleep and peace of mind, namely why I, unfortunately, like most victims of assault or abuse, never told anybody that I was being regularly abused.

When I began seriously considering this question, I initially identified various societal factors that were likely at play. This was the rural south in the 1970s, insular and self-protective in ways that you really had to experience to understand. Also, sexual abuse of children, generally, was not in the public's consciousness. To the contrary, communities often went to great lengths to shield offenders and otherwise pretend such things did not happen or, at least, happened somewhere else to somebody else's children. As Dr. Van Der Kolk observed:

> As Roland Summit wrote in his classic study *The Child Sexual Abuse Accommodation Syndrome* [published in 1983]: "Initiation, intimidation, stigmatization, isolation, helplessness and self-blame depend on a terrifying reality of child sexual abuse. Any attempts by the child to divulge the secret will be countered by an adult conspiracy of silence and disbelief. 'Don't worry about things like that; that could never happen in our family.' 'How could you ever think of such a terrible thing?' 'Don't let me hear you say anything like that again!' The average child never asks and never tells.'"

While these observations might explain why reporting my abuse may have accomplished little, they shed less light on why I was unable or unwilling to tell anybody what was happening to me. The answer seemingly lay elsewhere. While I had no real understanding of such things at the time, with hindsight and the passage of time, I now understand that the answer is in a sense straightforward and hardly unique to me. The shame, embarrassment, and powerlessness I experienced were likely sufficient to preclude action on my part. Add to that the fact that I felt (at least partially) responsible for the violence being visited upon me and my inaction was practically a metaphysical certainty.

Writing this is difficult because it seems just so incredibly absurd. Why in the world would a victim of sexual assault blame themselves for the abuse they suffered? My therapist scolded me for even pondering this question, offering instead a response which succinctly cut to the heart of the matter. As she said to me, "Who exactly *could* you tell? Every adult in your life failed you." Hard to argue with her observation, but I knew I still had not located a satisfactory answer.

Unfortunately, my response, or lack thereof to be accurate, is hardly unique. As researchers and therapists have come to realize, it is, in a very real sense, seemingly encoded in our DNA. Dr. Van Der Kolk explored this general phenomenon:

> Preoccupied with so many lingering questions about traumatic stress, I became intrigued with the idea that the nascent field of neuroscience could provide some answers and started to attend the meetings of the American College of Neuropsychopharmacology (ACNP). In 1984 the ACNP offered many fascinating lectures about drug development, but it was not until a few hours before my scheduled flight back to Boston that I heard a presentation by Steven Maier of the University of Colorado, who had collaborated with

Martin Seligman of the University of Pennsylvania. His topic was learned helplessness in animals. Maier and Seligman had repeatedly administered painful electric shocks to dogs who were trapped in locked cages. They called this condition "inescapable shock." Being a dog lover, I realized I could never have done such research myself, but I was curious about how this cruelty would affect the animals.

After administering several courses of electric shock, the researchers opened the doors of the cages and then shocked the dogs again. A group of control dogs who had never been shocked before immediately ran away, but the dogs who had earlier been subjected to inescapable shock made no attempt to flee, even when the door was wide open – they just lay there, whimpering and defecating. The mere opportunity to escape does not necessarily make traumatized animals, or people, take the road to freedom. Like Maier and Seligman's dogs, many traumatized people simply give up. Rather than risk experimenting with new options they stay stuck in the fear they know.

When I read this passage, I instantly understood, at a visceral level, why the dogs who had been subjected to "inescapable shock" did not get up and run away. As is sometimes observed, the devil you know is preferrable to the devil you don't know. As Dr. Van Der Kolk further observed:

> Further animal studies involving mice, rats, cats, monkeys, and elephants brought more intriguing data. For example, when researchers played a loud, intrusive sound, mice that had been raised in a warm nest with plenty of food scurried home immediately. But another group, raised in a noisy nest with scarce food supplies, also ran for home, even after spending time in more pleasant surroundings.
>
> Scared animals return home, regardless of whether home is safe or frightening. I thought about my patients with abusive families who kept going back to be hurt again. Are traumatized people condemned to seek refuge in what is familiar? If so, why, and is it possible to help them become attached to places and activities that are safe and pleasurable?

Articulating these insights slightly differently, Dr. McDonald gets to the heart of the matter:

> The truth is, sometimes we hold on to shame and blame because the alternative is *so much worse*. If you are sexually assaulted and believe you are

to blame for what happened, you also believe that preventing future assault is in your control. If it was your fault, you can prevent it in the future. If it is not your fault, then you have to accept that to be human is to be vulnerable to harm. If it is not your fault, the signpost that reads "bad things only happen to bad people" has to be replaced with one that reads, "there is senseless evil in the world." Given the option of two painful pills, one will likely choose the least painful one to swallow. Shame, though corrosive, is containable. The lesson that life is terrifying is not.

For close to 50 years, I have expended a great deal of mental energy exploring this question. What my therapist's response, and Dr. McDonald's and Dr. Van Der Kolk's insights, forced me to do was consider the question instead from the perspective of the child who was being repeatedly abused. Examined this way, my inaction is not surprising and, unfortunately, all too common.

When a man is prey to his emotions, he
is not his own master.

Benedict De Spinoza

The transition to becoming a teenager is difficult
enough for most kids under the best circumstances.
What does that experience look like for an extremely
dysregulated child who generally views the world as
incredibly dangerous and inhospitable? Funny you
should ask.

At home, I would constantly argue with and/or
outright defy my mother and Harvey, usually in
incredibly salty and disrespectful terms. Harvey,
being an old school "spare the rod, spoil the child"
type, occasionally tried to literally beat the
opposition and defiance out of me. This only made
me more determined to oppose and defy anything
and everything he and my mother demanded of me.
Conflict of this magnitude, however, can only be
maintained for so long.

While my mother and Harvey had many other
responsibilities and claims to their time and energy,
I was consumed by a singular desire, fueled by anger
and pain, to continue this fight indefinitely. In the
absence of any support or assistance, this was
seemingly my only way of communicating, albeit
quite badly, what I was feeling and experiencing.

Apparently sensing my willingness, and almost need, to escalate the conflict to Defcon-1[4] if necessary, Harvey and my mother essentially gave up the fight. There was no formal surrender, merely an implied détente. Certain territory was conceded and so long as I refrained from further (or at least excessive) hostilities, my gains would be implicitly recognized. While their decision to throw in the towel is perhaps understandable, it is nevertheless disappointing because they weren't simply giving up the fight they were, in effect, giving up on me.

Matters at school took a similar tack as I had quickly become an outsized management and discipline problem. I certainly can't defend the various ways in which I was disruptive and disrespectful, however, here again, most (if not all) of my behavior had its genesis in the ways my body was responding and reacting to the chaos and trauma it had endured.

Children experiencing dysregulation or hyperarousal of their stress response systems are often incorrectly perceived as suffering from one or more psychological disorders. As Dr. Perry observes,

---

[4] DEFCON, an acronym for Defense Condition, is the ranking system utilized by the United States military for defense readiness for a potential nuclear attack. DEFCON-5 reflects that conditions are "peacetime normal." DEFCON-1, on the other hand, represents the highest level of readiness for nuclear war and reflects that nuclear war is imminent or already under way.

"[i]n a classroom setting. . .hyperarousal responses look remarkably like attention deficit disorder, hyperactivity, or oppositional-defiant disorder. . .Hyperaroused youth can look hyperactive or inattentive because what they are attending to is the teacher's tone of voice or the other children's body language, not the content of their lessons."

To understand why this is the case, understand that the brain can be organized into several parts which vary in function and complexity. The simplest part of the brain, the brainstem, in part, manages our body's core regulatory functions. At the opposite end of the function and complexity spectrum is the cortex which manages high-level functions such as language and abstract thought.

Sensory input is processed by our brain from the bottom up beginning with our "lizard brain." As Dr. Perry explains, "[t]his means that before any new experience has a chance to be considered by the higher 'thinking' part of the brain, the lower brain has already interpreted and responded to it." In other words, "[a]ll the rational thoughts from our cortex have to get through the emotional filters of the lower brain."

If two reasonably well-regulated people attempt to communicate, this processing model presents little difficulty and they can communicate rationally, "cortex to cortex." On the other hand, if you attempt to communicate with someone who is experiencing dysregulation, "nothing you say will really get to their cortex, and nothing in their cortex will be easy for them to access." This is because the emotions associated with dysregulation, such as frustration, anger, and fear, can "shut down parts of the cortex." Thus, when someone is experiencing dysregulation, "they simply cannot use the smartest part of their brain" and their brain doesn't necessarily receive or perceive the words someone is speaking because their cortex, the part of the brain which manages higher-order functions such as language, simply isn't online. However, this does not mean that the dysregulated person's brain isn't receiving and processing sensory input. Quite the contrary, it's just that the dysregulated person's brain is focused on more emotional (or lower-order) input like tone of voice, facial expressions, and other non-verbal behavior. As Dr. Van Der Kolk observes:

> Abused kids are often very sensitive to changes in voices and faces, but they tend to respond to them as threats rather than cues for staying in sync. Dr. Seth Pollak of the University of Wisconsin showed a series of faces to a group of normal eight-year-olds and compared their responses with those of a group of abused children the same age. Looking at this spectrum of angry to sad expressions, the abused kids were hyperalert to the slightest features of anger. This is one reason abused children so easily become defensive or scared.

As a result, attempts to communicate with a dysregulated person can be frustrating and unproductive because the dysregulated person is listening for and hearing a very different "language." Thus, what was often perceived as inattention or defiance on my part was simply my brain's difficulty understanding what was trying to be communicated to me and/or my inability to "access" the more rational part of my brain. Let me put this in slightly less abstract terms.

I'm sure we've all watched television shows depicting environments such as the African veldt and its various animal life. Think of the gazelles, for example, existing in close proximity to numerous predators. The gazelles always seem a bit jumpy and are constantly scanning the environment for threats. They know they are prey and if they sense a threat (perceived or real), they don't engage in a measured cortex-based, high function, analysis. It's lizard brain, fight or flight, time. That is how I have experienced the world for far too much of my life. Far too many of my early experiences taught me, and hard wired into my brain, the conclusion that the world is a dangerous place filled with predators and generally inhospitable people and circumstances all conspiring to do me harm. Keep your head on a swivel and trust nothing and nobody.

I'm far less gazelle-like these days, but I haven't entirely shed this perception of the world (and probably never will). I'm still far more defensive and untrusting of the world than is generally warranted. My head is always on a swivel and I am far more cognizant than most of my surroundings. I am much more attuned than most to facial expressions, body language, and other non-verbal behavior. To this day, I often do not hear or fully comprehend what people say to me because I am instinctively focused on so many things other than the words they are speaking. These behaviors are too ingrained at a fundamental level (and I'm too old) to have much confidence that they will completely be eradicated from my system.

Considering just how badly dysregulated I was and, therefore, how defensively and/or aggressively I responded to far too many people and situations, it isn't surprising that I was such a discipline and management problem for my teachers. Because rural Alabama in the 1970s still firmly believed in corporal punishment, I received more than my fair share of paddlings. I was also suspended more times that I can recall for a variety of defiant, unruly, and just plain anti-social behavior.[5]

Eventually, my teachers and other school officials realized the truth in the adage, "never wrestle with a pig - you both get dirty and the pig likes it." Their

---

[5] A representative sampling (a tasting menu of sorts) of some of my transgressions include (1) dropping a seemingly endless (and not uncreative) string of f-bombs on a bewildered teacher, (2) publicly (and repeatedly) making another teacher the punch line of an incredibly offensive joke, and (3) punching a girl in the mouth, repeatedly, because when told to "shut up," she replied, "make me."

solution was to simply deprive me of the confrontation and conflict I seemingly craved. Rather than feed my rage through confrontation, my teachers decided to "starve the beast," as it were, making me sit in the hallway by myself or otherwise isolating me. They seemingly didn't care what I did, so long as I did it out of sight and earshot.

It is amazing the extent to which anger, hurt, and pain can fuel someone forward, but even the brightest stars eventually burn out and collapse inward on themselves. Likewise, my desire and/or ability to engage with the world, albeit destructively and ineffectively, just sort of burned out. Rather than fight a battle with pain and disorientation I could neither identify nor assuage, I opted for a different approach. If I could not defeat or quiet what was raging inside me, perhaps I could numb it into submission.

Thus, began a span of several years in which my relationship with alcohol was about as unhealthy and dangerous as possible. To paraphrase Russell Brand's infamous quote on the subject, however, I didn't have a drinking problem - I had a reality problem and drinking was my solution. Shockingly, attempting to numb myself out of existence didn't turn out to be much of a solution. That I survived the experience was not from a lack of effort on my part, however. I eventually reached a point where getting blackout drunk on the weekends was the norm and I experienced on more than one occasion alcohol poisoning that could have, and, quite frankly, should have, finished me. Also, that I managed not to kill myself or others from behind the wheel is an enduring mystery.

You may find yourself wondering how I was able to get my mitts on alcohol at such a young age. I suspect that it has always been relatively easy for kids to get their hands on alcohol if they know who to ask and where to look. This certainly was the case for me, although the specific circumstances and methods may seem foreign to some, especially in the 21st century.

The rural south of my youth embodied a great many contradictions. Such was on full display when it came to alcohol. Whisky was a food group and beer was holy water, but God forbid that such sinful products be available for easy purchase. Alabama in the 1970s, with the exception of a few isolated – and distant – counties, was dry as dirt. To those unfamiliar with the concept, a "dry county" is one in which alcohol cannot be legally purchased.

These descendants of rebellion, however, were not about to let the government so flagrantly violate their inalienable right to be free from sobriety. So, enter the local bootlegger. To the uninitiated, a bootlegger was an entrepreneur who sold alcohol out of his house or, more frequently in my environs, his mobile home. Understanding the importance of customer service, most bootleggers even offered some form of drive-thru service, so you could get your beer or liquor without ever leaving the comfort of your vehicle.

There is much that could be written about bootleggers, how this black-market economy worked and why the police never seemed particularly interested in shutting them down. Simply put, however, if you had a vehicle, were willing to pay the inflated prices (i.e., the "bootlegger's tax"), and were known to the bootlegger, or his or her family, purchasing alcohol was as easy as rolling through the Burger King drive-thru.

Being a young transplant from north of the Mason-Dixon line, I lacked both a vehicle and the community recognition to purchase alcohol on my own. However, I had several friends who easily satisfied these requirements.[6] As for the bootlegger's tax, it was offset by the fact that at our age it simply didn't require all that much alcohol to get our buzz on.

At this age, our "parties" were boringly uncreative. I would usually spend the weekend with one of my friends where we would be picked up by another friend who had a car. We would then spend several hours mostly just riding around, drinking and carrying on. Sometimes, we'd spend the weekend at the house of somebody whose parents were away

---

[6] One of the benefits, at least to me, of the piss-poor state of Alabama's educational system was that more than a few poorly performing kids were held back one (or more) grades. Thus, it was not that difficult for me to find friends who were old enough to drive as they often were sitting within arm's reach.

just hanging out, drinking and carrying on. Eventually, no longer content to drink just on the weekends, I started drinking to celebrate the coming day of educational futility. I usually rode to school with a couple friends and along the way we would often drink beer or have a couple shots of whatever was available. I later just started carrying beer into homeroom in a Hardee's cup. I'd just sit there, zoned out, drinking beer through a straw.

When I turned 16 and got a car, I felt like a prisoner who had just been paroled. Getting a car at 16 was an absolute right of passage in the rural south of my youth. There was no easier way to be ostracized than to turn 16 and not have a car (or at least easy access to a car). Undoubtedly preferring that I be able to freely go where I wanted and, therefore, not be at home, my mother bought me a piece-of-shit '64 Nova for my 16th birthday. It should probably come as no surprise that it took me less than one month to be arrested and charged with reckless driving and possession of alcohol.[7]

---

[7] The arresting officers' uncertainty whether I had resisted arrest (see box 33) still makes me laugh. I absolutely tried to resist. My effort was apparently so weak, however, that what I was trying to accomplish didn't even fully register.

CIIC-34 Rev. 5/77

ALABAMA UNIFORM ARREST REPORT

1. SID NO.	SID	2. FBI NO.	FBI	3. Contributor's ORI	4. Agency Name	5. Agency Case No. OCA
				AL 0 3 3 0 V D 0	RUSSELLVILLE P.D.	8 0 - 2 5

6. Last Name	First	Middle	7. Alias AKA	
AMBROSE	RUSSELL	DAVID		

8. SEX	9. RAC	10. HGT	11. WGT	12. EYE	13. HAI	14. SKN	15. Scars, Marks, Tattoos and Amputations	SMT
M	W	6 Ft. 0 In.	140	Blue	BRO	FAIR		

16. Place of Birth (City-Town-County)	POB	17. State	18. Social Sec. No.	SOC	19. Date of Birth	DOB	20. Miscellaneous No. (Indicate type)
JACKSON		mic			Month 03 Day 04 Year 64		

21. Fingerprint Class (Leave Blank) FPC		Key	Major	Primary	Scdy.	Sub-Secondary	Final	22. Identification Comments	ICO
HENRY CLASS		H Y							
NCIC CLASS									

23. Home Address Street	City-Town-County	State	24. Res. Phone	25. Occupation (Be Specific)
Rt #3 Box 259A Phil Campbell		AL.	993-4500	Student

26. Employer (Name of Company or School)	27. Business Address (Street-City-State)	28. Bus. Phone
Russellville Senior High	Russellville, AL.	

29. Location of Arrest (Street-City-State)	30. Sector Number	31. Arrested for your Jurisdiction?
		☐ Yes ☐ Other Ala. Agency ☐ Out-of-State

32. Condition of Arrestee	33. Resist Arrest?	34. Injuries?	35. Armed?	36. Description of Weapon
☐ 1. Drunk ☐ 3. Narcotic ☐ 2. Drinking ☑ Sober	☐ Yes ☑ No	☐ Officer ☐ Arrestee	☐ Yes ☑ No	

37. Date of Arrest OOA	38. Time of Arrest	39. B T M W F	40. Type Arrest	41. Arrested Before?
Month 03 Day 29 Year 80	9:18		☑ On-View ☐ Cell ☐ Warrant	☐ Yes ☐ No ☑ Unk.

42. Charge - 1	AOL	A. Offense Date DOO	48. Charge - 2	AOL	A. Offense Date DOO
Unlawful Possession of Alcoholic		0 3 2 9 80	Reckless Driving		0 3 29 80

43. NCIC Code	AON	44.	B. Time of Offense	49. NCIC Code	AON	50.	B. Time of Offense
		Beverages ☑ Misd. ☐ Felony	9:18			☑ Misd. ☐ Felony	9:18

45. State Statute Citation CIT	46. Warrant No.	47. Date Issued	51. State Statute Citation CIT	52. Warrant No.	53. Date Issued
					03 29 80

54. Charge - 3		A. Offense Date DOO	60. Charge - 4		A. Offense Date DOO

55. NCIC Code	AON	56.	B. Time of Offense	61. NCIC Code	AON	62.	B. Time of Offense
		☐ Misd. ☐ Felony				☐ Misd. ☐ Felony	

57. State Statute Citation CIT	58. Warrant No.	59. Date Issued	63. State Statute Citation CIT	64. Warrant No.	65. Date Issued

OBTS No. A- 0718757	66. Arrest Disposition ☐ 1. Held ☐ 2. Relsd. ☐ 3. TOT-LE ☐ 4. Bail ☐ 5. TOT-JV ☐ 6. REF-JUV ☐ 7. Other	67. If out on Release, what type?	68. Additional Arrest Disposition ADD

69. Arrested with (1) Accomplice Full Name	70. Arrested with (2) Accomplice Full Name

71. Veh. Yr.	72. Vehicle Make	73. Veh. Mod.	74. Style	75. (Top) (Bottom)	76. Tag No.	77. State	78. Yr.

79. V.I.N.	80. Impounded? ☐ Yes ☐ No	81. Location

82. Other Evidence Seized (Court Papers in Arrestee's Possession?)

83. Circumstances Leading to, or Resulting in, Arrest. Include Disposition of Items Seized. (Describe Bri...

Continue on Back

84. Arresting Officer - 1 (Last Name-First-Middle)	85. Code No.	86. Arresting Officer - 2 (Last Name-First-Middle)	87. Code No.
McGuire D.	79-9	Ivie V.	A-7

TYPE OR PRINT IN BLACK INK ONLY

By this time, my mother and Harvey had divorced and my mother had begun the quest for husband number four. Thus distracted, my mother rarely attempted to exert any real control or authority over me. I wanted to be anywhere but home and having a car afforded me the opportunity to essentially go wherever I wanted, whenever I wanted.

Even had she wanted to assume the role of parent, it would have been difficult for her to do so because she was spending more and more time away from home in search of husband number four. Not impressed with the available men-folk in our local area, my mother began spending more and more time in the Huntsville-Decatur area, more than an hour's drive away.

Sometime in early 1981, my mother met Wilbur Stevens, who lived in Decatur. By the time that summer rolled around, things between the two had become serious. So much so that my mother (and my sister) spent practically the entire summer at Wilbur's place. In the general absence of any adult (or pseudo-adult) supervision, I continued to wild-out as much as possible. When my mother would occasionally return home, she would comically (and futilely) attempt to assert her authority. By this point, I had zero respect for my mother and had no intention of complying with any request or adhering to any rule she might impose. As far as I was concerned, my mother had long ago forfeited her parental authority. My mother, likewise, had reached her limit because it was toward the end of that summer that she petitioned the court to be relieved of any further responsibility for my care. As previously noted, the court, having adjudicated me an ungovernable and incorrigible CHINS, granted my mother's request.

While I was relieved to be free, officially and legally, of my mother, the rest of the court's order was less agreeable. I was hardly in a position to live on my own, so the court had to place me somewhere, at least until I completed my final year of high school. The court, however, rather than place me with a responsible adult, ordered that I reside with Harvey, my mother's third husband, the man whose friend subjected me to many months of abuse. I certainly had no intention of recognizing or respecting the authority of the man who, in my mind, facilitated and implicitly condoned my abuse.

<table>
<tr><td>State of Alabama
Unified Judicial System
Dept. of Court Mgmt.
Form C-18 Rev 8/77</td><td>ORDER</td><td>Case Number
JU 81 348
ID YR Number</td></tr>
</table>

IN THE   DISTRICT JUVENILE   COURT OF   FRANKLIN   COUNTY

Plaintiff   vs Defendant

In The Matter Of: RUSSELL DAVID AMBROSE
(Juvenile Case)

Temporary physical custody of Russell David Ambrose is hereby placed with Harvey Mason, with legal custody remaining with the child's natural mother, Nancy Mason. Mr. Mason is hereby given the right to enroll child in school and sign any documents necessary to effectuate his school enrollment and the power to seek emergency medical treatment as necessary.

Done and Ordered this the 14th day of August, 1981.

J. W. Gilliland, District Juvenile Judge

Certified As A True Copy

81/18/81
Date

Signature of Clerk/Register

Signature of Judge/Clerk/Register

Harvey, however, was intent on bringing me to heel and true to his character approached the situation as if I were a wild horse over which he could gain compliance through violence and force of will. This was guaranteed to end badly. Sure enough, it didn't take long for us to come to blows. More precisely, my mouth continued writing checks my ass couldn't cash and Harvey decided to collect the overdraft fee with his fists. I quickly realized I had two – and only two – options: (1) complete surrender and total compliance or (2) escape. While some version of the former was what I probably needed, I'm not sure anybody – least of all Harvey – could have gotten through to me or gained any sort of control over me. At that point, I simply wasn't capable of anything even remotely resembling compliance or submission to authority. Factor in the hatred and distrust I felt for Harvey and this was a "gots to go" situation. So, I left.

For the next several months I was in the wind. While I technically did not have a "home," I wasn't exactly "homeless." I occasionally slept in my car or at the Hardees where I worked, but most of the time I was able to stay with friends. I had a small handful of friends whose parents had some vague intuition of my circumstance and were willing to let me stay for 2-3 nights at a time. So, I would rotate from one friend's house to another with an occasional break to sleep at work or in my car. It was not so much being homeless but more like somebody in witness protection being shuttled from safe house to safe house.

Initially, Harvey didn't seem to take action to find me or take me back into custody. Perhaps he realized that, at least for the time being, it was prudent to just stand down. Also, because this was a small town where everybody seemed to know everybody else's business, he may have learned that I usually had a safe place to stay. Eventually, however, Harvey submitted a petition to the court characterizing me as a "runaway" and seeking my return.

State of Alabama Supreme Court Dept. of Court Mgmt. Form JU-8 1-77	**PETITION**	Case Number JU **83** **041** ID YR Number

IN THE JUVENILE COURT OF _____ FRANKLIN _____ COUNTY

In the Matter of: _____ Russell "Rusty" Ambrose _____ (DOB-3-14-64) , a child under the age of 18
My name is _____ Harvey Mason _____ I am over 19 years of age.
My address is _____ Rt. 7, Russellville, Alabama _____
My occupation is _____ Pest Control _____

Child's Name _____ Russell Ambrose _____
Child's Address _____ same as above _____

Child's Father _____ Jim Ambrose _____
Address _____ India _____

Child's Mother _____ Helen Ambrose _____
Address _____ Lake City, S. C. _____

Child's Guardian or Physical Custodian _____ Harvey Mason _____
Address _____ same as above _____

Guardianship, custody, control and supervision of the child is vested _____ Harvey Mason _____

The said child is ☐ Delinquent, ☐ Dependant, ☒ In need of supervision
in that _he has left leaving no address and not telling him where he was going_

The said child is also in immediate or threatened danger of physical and/or emotional harm in that
I know nothing about the circumstances surrounding the place where he is staying--
he may be in danger-- he needs to be where his guardian knows to reach him

and he should be removed immediately.

☐ Affidavit Attached

I swear that I am informed and believe and state upon such information, knowledge, and belief, that the above allegations and facts are true.

1-3-82
Date

Harvey Mason
Signature

Intake Officer

Had I been attending school I would have been easy to locate. By this time, however, high school was long in my rearview mirror. I didn't see the point, so I just stopped attending and began hanging out with (and eventually living with) some friends I worked with who had already completed (or likewise given up on) school. By the time anybody seemed to notice (or care) that I was no longer attending school, I had missed so many days and so much work that even attempting to catch up so that I could graduate just didn't seem worth the effort. So, in the spring of 1982, shortly after turning 18, I officially quit school. Later that spring, I obtained my GED.

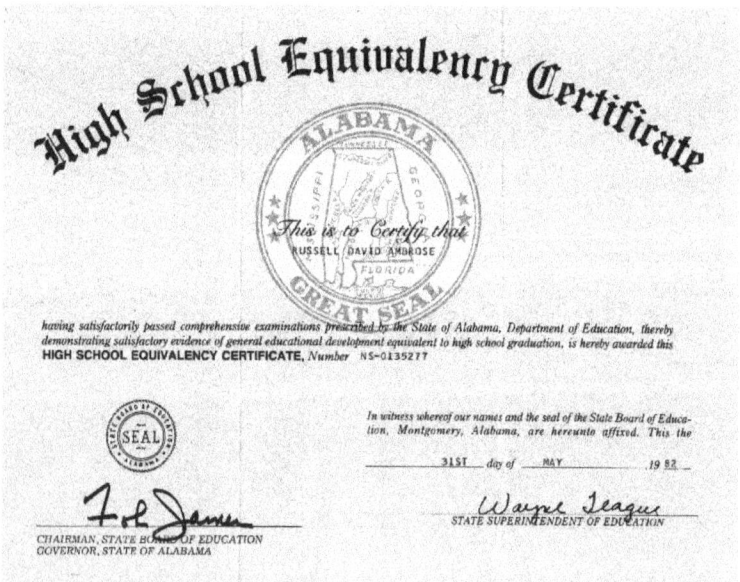

High School Equivalency Certificate

This is to Certify that
RUSSELL DAVID AMBROSE

having satisfactorily passed comprehensive examinations prescribed by the State of Alabama, Department of Education, thereby demonstrating satisfactory evidence of general educational development equivalent to high school graduation, is hereby awarded this **HIGH SCHOOL EQUIVALENCY CERTIFICATE**, Number NS-0135277

In witness whereof our names and the seal of the State Board of Education, Montgomery, Alabama, are hereunto affixed. This the

_31ST_ day of _MAY_ , 19 82

STATE SUPERINTENDENT OF EDUCATION

CHAIRMAN, STATE BOARD OF EDUCATION
GOVERNOR, STATE OF ALABAMA

Salva made up his mind. He would walk south, to Kenya. He did not know what he would find once he got there, but it seemed to be his best choice.

Linda Sue Park, *A Long Walk to Water*

Let's take a brief time out and take stock of where my life was in the summer of 1982. Considering the sheer amount of stupid and self-destructive behavior in which I had thus far engaged, that I was still alive was a minor miracle. I was unable to earn a high school diploma and had been officially declared too unruly to walk around unsupervised. This circumstance would have been bad enough had I lived among a highly educated and well-mannered people. However, when you consider that Alabama routinely has the 49th or 50th ranked education system in the United States and its citizens are a rowdy bunch who think the Dukes of Hazard are role models second only to Jesus himself, my "accomplishments" take on a special luster.

To put it mildly, I was adrift, literally and figuratively. I barely knew where my next meal was coming from and I certainly seemed to be on the fast-track to a meaningless, dead-end existence. . .or worse. In short, my luck – and my options – were quickly running out. While I was at a complete loss how to accomplish it, I knew I wanted something different for my life. The only thing I seemed to grasp was that if I was to have any chance at something different I would absolutely have to physically remove myself from the great state of Alabama. Literally get away from the people and situations that were in the way of me (hopefully) figuring out how to get my shit together.

Enter the United States Air Force. I would like to say that I enlisted out of a sense of duty and/or patriotism, but the reality is that it was, to my mind, my best (and possibly last) chance at escaping my likely fate. The truth is, at that juncture, I was open to just about any possibility, including alien abduction, so long as it allowed me to physically remove myself from my then present location and circumstance.

I selected the Air Force because it guaranteed that I would be trained as a photographer which sounded like fun. Joining the Air Force and moving to a completely different part of the country away from the world I knew seemed to be a good decision. I was provided structure…LOL…I had structure forced on me by the United States government. So, why was I willing to generally accept, albeit often quite grudgingly, the structure and discipline imposed on me by Uncle Sam? In at least one sense, the answer is pretty straightforward. I absolutely knew that if I washed out, I would have been shipped back to Alabama to endure an almost certain fate. While I was still very much "lost," one thing I was certain of was that I never wanted to set foot in Alabama, literally or figuratively, ever again. In a sense, I was channeling my inner Hernán Cortes.[8] I was

---

[8] Hernán Cortes was the Spanish conquistador who conquered the Aztecs and claimed Mexico for the

venturing forth into new territory and failure was simply not an option.

After basic training, the Air Force sent me to film school at Lowry AFB outside of Denver. Film school was a blast. I got along pretty well with the small group in my training class and for roughly six months, I got to travel around Denver, Boulder, and Colorado Springs photographing a variety of people, animals, and locations. This was all long before the age of digital photography, so I also got to play around in the dark room for hours on end developing my own film and creating my own photographs. The cherry-on-top of this experience was when fate placed me courtside, underneath the basket with camera in hand, for the 1984 NBA All-Star game in Denver.

Spanish Empire. Cortes is perhaps most known for scuttling his ships upon landing on the Mexican coast. Cortes' message to his army was simple – prevail or die. Likewise, I instinctively understood the cost if I failed to fully grasp and breathe life into this opportunity.

34TH NBA ALL-STAR GAME
JANUARY 29, 1984   DENVER, COLORADO
TM

Sunday, January 29, 1984
12:00 Noon

PHOTO PASS

MEDIA BRUNCH

I was still very much learning about photography and didn't have particularly good gear. Nevertheless, I was able to get a few pretty solid shots including this gem of Larry Bird with Dr. J in the background.

After film school, I was sent to Offutt AFB near Omaha where I spent the rest of my enlistment working in an underground film vault primarily creating different visual products, mostly from satellite imagery, for various "customers" within the military and intelligence community.[9]

This work may sound interesting, and I suppose it was for a time, but the reality was much more mundane. While I had a Top Secret-SCI clearance[10] and, therefore, access to sensitive information, it never felt like I was seeing or working with anything all that sexy or important. This was largely because I generally had only a vague understanding of the individual puzzle piece I was creating or working with. I rarely saw the finished product into which my efforts went and, therefore, had little

---

[9] Offutt AFB was, at the time, headquarters for the Strategic Air Command (SAC), the military command then responsible for the aircraft and intercontinental ballistic missile (ICBM) components of the United States' nuclear arsenal. SAC was also responsible for reconnaissance aircraft such as the U-2 and SR-71. SAC was discontinued as a major command in the early 1990s as part of a military re-organization and its missions and functions assigned elsewhere.

[10] That the government granted me a Top Secret security clearance is still a head-scratcher. I think when they investigated my background they went to Albania instead of Alabama. I can't imagine the people I actually grew up with telling the government anything that could reasonably cause them to conclude, "yeah, this guy is solid, let's let him play around with Top Secret stuff."

understanding of the larger context. In a sense, I helped produce widgets. Granted, they were Top Secret widgets but I didn't have much sense of how these particular widgets fit into the bigger picture. There was, however, one memorable exception.

In the Spring of 1986, I was working the night shift which I really enjoyed. At night, the lab was almost always empty of officers and "management" (a.k.a. non-workers). With very few exceptions, the only people in the lab overnight were lower-ranking enlistees, free to get work done without all the bullshit that seemingly occupied far too much of the daylight hours.

Early one morning around 2 a.m., a small group of people, including several officers, entered the lab looking puzzled and speaking in low voices. This was very unusual because our "customers" *rarely* visited the lab. We were located on the opposite side of the base from SAC HQ in a vault (literally) which required special access to enter. Regardless, we went to work. We were given the relevant information and instructed to create several large transparencies. We had no idea what the fuss was about but did as ordered. We were used to producing photos and transparencies of anything and everything. There wasn't time to stare at our work product to try and figure out what was there. Create the requested product, send it on its way, and move on to the next assignment.

It was rare when we were able to watch folks take our raw photo product and analyze it. So, we were interested when our visitors took the transparencies we created and instead of just leaving the lab to conduct analysis somewhere else, laid everything out on our light tables and began examining the scene with their magnifying devices. Perhaps sensing our curiosity, a Major called us over. He handed one of us his magnifier, pointed to a particular spot on the transparency, and said, "what do you see?" We looked where the Major had directed but all we could see was what looked like an unusually damaged structure in the vicinity of several industrial buildings. So, we told him we didn't know what was there. I'll never forget his response, "we don't what's there either, but there was a nuclear reactor there yesterday." Because there was no internet in 1986, news and information didn't travel very fast. So, we had no idea to what the Major was referring. However, we were able to piece it together soon enough when Russia (finally) acknowledged that there had been an incident at one of the Chernobyl nuclear reactors. I then realized that I had processed, and been one of the first people to examine, satellite imagery of the Chernobyl disaster long before the world at large knew of this incident.

Ultimately, I served in the Air Force for just under six years[11] and while I often chafed under the discipline and conformity, it was a positive experience and I was honorably discharged. Again,

---

[11] It was a six-year enlistment, but once I made the decision not to re-enlist the Air Force sent me on my way a few months early.

aside from two unique experiences my tenure as an Airman was fairly unremarkable. This is not to say that my life *outside* of the photo lab was boring or uneventful. To the contrary, some of the most significant events in my life occurred during this time.

Your mental illness was kind of like
your middle name. I didn't know what
it was, but I knew that you had one.

Taylor Tomlinson

My wife, Lisa, and I have been married almost 25
years. What very few folks know, however, is that
Lisa represents my second (and final) effort at
matrimony. I very rarely mention or think about my
first marriage. It seemingly happened a lifetime ago
and was sort of like a solar eclipse – brief and intense
with the very real threat of permanent damage if not
approached safely or properly.

After being transferred to Nebraska, it took some
time to adjust to my new surroundings and routines
as well as my odd work schedule. After living in the
barracks for about 12 months, I moved off-base into
an apartment in Omaha. This helped me begin
meeting a few non-military people. I eventually met
a young woman, Danita, and she and I began a
relationship somewhere between hanging out and
dating. I think we both viewed the other as a mildly
fun distraction until something better came along.
Be careful what you wish for.

One afternoon, Danita picked me up and told me we
were going to pick up one of her friends. When told
we were picking up her friend at a psychiatric
hospital, I just assumed Danita's friend *worked*
there. Nope. Danita's friend was a long-term in-

patient at the facility and had been given an afternoon pass.[12]

As Calvin Candie famously quipped, "you had my curiosity, but now you have my attention." I had lived with a few people who should have been patients in a psychiatric hospital, but never before had I met anybody who actually *lived* in one. I'm not really sure what I expected, but whatever I might have expected was most certainly not what I encountered that afternoon.

The facility was busy that afternoon with quite a few people coming and going. When Cynthia Hamilton walked out of the facility, I assumed she was an employee or similar professional. She was attractive, fashionably dressed with well-done hair and make-up. . .and she was headed straight for Danita's car.

As soon as Cynthia got into the car, I began peppering her with questions. Almost immediately, of course, I asked her why she was living at a psychiatric hospital.[13] Beyond this, I don't recall

---

[12] I later learned this was not the first in-patient stay for Danita's friend. It would also not be her last.

[13] Cynthia suffers from Bi-Polar Disorder. When I met Cynthia, the pharmacological options for treating this disease were much more limited. Cynthia was subsequently prescribed lithium and while it was occasionally effective, lithium is notoriously difficult to dose which made sustained improvement for Cynthia elusive during this time.

specifically what we discussed but I do recall that I was a tad rude and nosy. I simply would not let her be. I was intrigued and once I realized that Cynthia shared my very dark and cynical sense of humor and was, to boot, quite intelligent, I was smitten. I didn't get the sense that Cynthia shared my smitten-ness, but she did appear to exhibit some occasional glimmers of interest between expressions of general frustration with my antics.

From my perspective, that afternoon went well and only increased my interest in seeing Cynthia again. Shockingly, however, I was not invited to participate in any of Cynthia's subsequent respites from treatment. Cynthia was, however, discharged from the hospital not too long after our encounter and as luck would have it, Danita and Cynthia worked together at a shopping mall department store. While I dislike shopping and shopping malls, I made an exception in this circumstance.

Over the course of the next several weeks I visited Danita at work, usually at times when Cynthia was also working. Cynthia gradually warmed to my attention and eventually made sure to let me know when she would be working. It didn't take long for me to completely lose track of Danita's work schedule, giving me the opportunity to visit Cynthia without any pretense of interest in somebody else.

Danita, realizing my growing interest in Cynthia, and having never been terribly interested in me, was perfectly happy to play match-maker. Unbeknownst to me, as part of this effort, Danita provided Cynthia with my address. Cynthia did not wait long before stopping by, unannounced, at my apartment. After several minutes of meaningless chatter, Cynthia blurted out, "you can kiss me now, if you want." Thus began a relationship characterized by a level of dysfunction and chaos that would have made my mother proud.

Here on Earth, the distance between heaven and hell is the difference between faith and doubt.

Val Kilmer

Joining the Air Force provided a measure of structure and purpose and helped to dial down a bit my worst self-destructive tendencies. However, that my tendency toward reckless, irresponsible, and self-destructive behavior had lessened, did not mean that the underlying problems driving such behavior had dissipated or lessened in severity. To the contrary, the troubles roiling through my system, like kudzu left unchecked, found even greater purchase and continued to expand and interfere with my ability to enjoy life.

Moreover, while my budding relationship with Cynthia supplied some welcomed levity and distraction, it provided no real help for what was continuing to eat at me. To the contrary, our relationship, more often than not, exacerbated our worst tendencies and presented an impediment to any real personal improvement. Thus, my subconscious desire to find some measure of escape from this life certainly did not abate. What eventually changed, however, was my approach. Simply put, having failed to find relief, indirectly, through poor decision making and self-destructive behavior, I eventually explored more direct avenues of relief.

The transition, if you will, from indirect self-destructive behavior to actively contemplating ending my life was neither sudden nor, initially, even noticeable. It was not an instantaneous change in my outlook or thought process but was instead more like a virus which slowly spread throughout my system gradually weakening my resistance to its promise. This was obviously not healthy thinking but, to be fair, I was far from healthy and this virus eventually overtook my system.

Spoiler Alert - I did not, ultimately, take my own life. Thus, I can imagine somebody saying to themselves, "if dude had really wanted to kill himself, he would have actually done it." Fair enough, but this observation badly misunderstands the nature of what I was experiencing. It wasn't so much that I wanted to die, I was simply tired of living. I was exhausted trying to navigate a world for which I was seemingly so ill-equipped. I had simply grown tired carrying around – and being assaulted by – pain I could neither identify nor manage.

It is difficult to articulate what I was experiencing, primarily because, in a sense, I was being assaulted in a foreign language. Dr Van Der Kolk's description of how traumatic memories are processed by the body is well stated:

> We remember insults and injuries best. The adrenaline that we secrete to defend against potential threats helps to engrave those incidents into our minds. . .[t]he more adrenaline you

secrete, the more precise your memory will be. But that is true only up to a certain point. Confronted with horror – especially the horror of 'inescapable shock' – this system becomes overwhelmed and breaks down. . .At this point the emotional brain, which is not under conscious control and cannot communicate in words, takes over. The emotional brain (the limbic area and the brain stem) expresses its altered activation through changes in emotional arousal, body physiology, and muscular action. . .As a result, the imprints of traumatic experiences are organized not as coherent logical narratives but in fragmented sensory and emotional traces: images, sounds, and physical sensations.

Moreover, as Dr. McDonald observes, "traumatic memories" are not, in fact, memories:

One of the biggest failures of the language of trauma is that we refer to traumatic memories as memories. As if they look or feel like all the rest of our memories. As if we had control over them. Traumatic memories are not memories; they are instances of unwilling and unbidden *reliving*. When we remember, we have cognitive control. We have access to the parts of our brain that can think rationally. And while we may feel some of the emotions related to the memory, we typically can put the memory and emotions away when we need to. Reliving, on the other hand, is not something we do, it is something that happens to us. It puts us back into the time of the trauma.

In short, time does not heal all wounds but often exacerbates and compounds them. Lacking the "life skills" to navigate what I was experiencing, and not knowing where to discover or how to develop them, I felt like I was quickly running out of options. Suicide was certainly not something I *desired*, it was simply the option which eventually appeared the most viable. So, having secured the means to end my life and confident this was the best course of action, I was (I thought) prepared to carry this endeavor to its conclusion.

Having arrived at this conclusion, I experienced a peace of mind I had never before experienced (and have rarely, if at all, experienced since). Just as escape appeared inevitable, however, some part of my system, sensing the reality of the situation, instinctively began to fight back in a desperate effort to save itself. It was literally as if something in my system, too long dormant, decided to finally assert itself. What I thought would be a relatively quick, and ultimately peaceful event, turned into an hours-long battle, internal and intensely personal, for my existence.

Once I decided to end my life and took concrete steps to secure this result, circumstances reached a critical mass and in a very real sense took on a life of their own. It was as if a final launch countdown had been initiated by one part of my system while a different part of my system was trying to figure out how to hack the network and abort the launch. This battle, while internal, was very real. Moreover, while it was not a physical battle in the traditional sense, it certainly manifested itself physically, including a sense of terror I hope to never again experience. Ultimately, after several hours of struggle, the part of me that wanted (or thought it wanted) to end its existence lost out.

Admittedly, my description of these events is oddly vague and melodramatic. The vagueness is, I suppose, intentional. I've never shared the specific events of that night with anybody and I'm not going to begin now. If you've stared into that abyss, you *know* what I experienced without me having to tell you. On the other hand, if you have never experienced that dark landscape first-hand, it is something which words are incapable of sufficiently conveying. As for the melodrama, I think it's hard to avoid as there may be fewer things more dramatic than securing the means to end your life with the conscious intent to do so. While I don't often think about the events of that night, I still have easy access to the memories. The scene is easily recalled and I can smell the room and feel the terror. The images are vivid and crystal clear. If anything, my description fails to do justice to the drama that played out that night.

Again, I did not consciously want to die, but I had completely lost the desire to live in a world in which I felt increasingly lost with incessant turmoil coursing through my system. So, if my dangerous flirtation with suicide was not because I consciously wanted to end my life, what the hell was I doing? I think most folks intuitively understand that I, like others that engage in similar behavior, was at least partially crying out for help in, sadly, the only language then available to me. This naturally begs the question whether my cry for help was answered and, if so, what did I do in response to such help?

We lie best when we lie to ourselves.

Stephen King

Pro tip – if you decide to flirt this seriously with suicide, but do not want your significant other to discover such, make sure that you did not meet your significant other at a psychiatric hospital. The day following my flirtation with suicide, Cynthia stopped over and as the kids might say, "game recognized game." She immediately intuited what had transpired the night before and where my head had been (and was at least partially still at apparently). Knowing all too well how to navigate the mental health infrastructure, Cynthia communicated with folks who, in very short order, stuffed my ass in an Air Force cargo plane headed west. Upon my arrival in Denver, I was transported to the Fitzsimons Army Medical Center for a few weeks of involuntary rest and relaxation.

Just as nobody expects the Spanish Inquisition, most people don't expect to be whisked away at a moment's notice to an inpatient psychiatric facility. While my initial impressions of the experience were benign, I was reminded, in short order, where I was. At some point during my first evening, I heard somebody screaming and carrying on. While it was nearly impossible to discern what this person was screaming, the raw, visceral nature of his outbursts was unmistakable.

Walking through the facility a short time later, I discovered the source of the disturbance. In one of the isolation rooms, a guy was strapped to a bed with four-point restraints. I later met Joe and learned he was suffering from paranoid schizophrenia. Despite being restrained, Joe was struggling mightily to free himself. He was also continuing to vocalize his displeasure with loud undecipherable outbursts. I still remember how disheartened I felt experiencing this, partly out of concern for Joe, but more so because I began to wonder just what in the hell I had gotten myself into. My concern only increased the following morning when Joe, appearing more zombie than human, had turned silent. I later learned that Joe had been subdued by a very large dose of Thorazine, a medication with which he was apparently intimately familiar.

My fears and concerns were soon largely dispelled, however. The staff seemed reasonable and most of the patients with whom I initially had contact were unthreatening. If anything, the atmosphere was much more docile and accommodating than I would ever have expected. It was less One Flew Over the Cuckoo's Nest, with severely disturbed and dangerous people, and more Breakfast Club, a relatively harmless gaggle of weird misfits experiencing tremendous difficulty navigating and managing the world around them.

After getting acclimated and demonstrating that I was not a threat to myself or others, a routine of sorts was established. We arose early and performed a variety of tedious tasks designed to remind us that we were, at least in theory, still in the military. Later in the morning, I met with the treatment staff who shared their impressions and observations while trying (without success) to get me to discuss what brought me there. I lied and told them I was not sure why I was there and that I was just tired and stressed out. I downplayed the events that led to my hospitalization, specifically asserting that I certainly had done nothing more than make some off-hand comments about suicide and certainly had not taken any concrete steps to actually end my life.

It is obvious with hindsight that I was lying to myself more than I was lying to the people trying to help me. I simply was not ready (or able) to be honest with myself or anybody else about what I had experienced or what I was feeling. Moreover, it was not simply that I was unwilling to discuss these things in a group setting because when I met privately with a psychologist, I lied to her as well.

One of the coping or survival skills I developed at an early age was the ability to adapt to my surroundings and circumstances. This is certainly what I did during my hospitalization. Looking back, I realize just how automatic this response was. I was not willing (or able) to explore what I had experienced or how it had impacted me, so I simply lied to myself and everybody around me in an effort to make my hospitalization as brief as possible. As my discharge summary put it, I "showed no evidence of significant moodiness or somatic vegetative symptoms of depression." Moreover, I "adapted quickly to the ward and related well to staff and patients. . .and within a week and a half was anxious to return to duty."

Having fooled myself and everybody around me, I was discharged after 24 days having failed to take advantage of the opportunity my hospitalization presented. Nevertheless, the experience was not without some benefit. Prior to the events that resulted in my hospitalization, suicide as a viable option was something I had long considered a possibility. It was rarely high on my to-do list, but never did I consider it to be an unacceptable option. Well, after my brief involuntary vacation, and the events leading up to such, suicide was eliminated - permanently - from my vocabulary. There was nothing about this experience I ever wanted to repeat or re-live, so a different approach would have to be explored.

Having ruled out suicide, I had, generally speaking, two options for dealing with what was eating me from the inside: (1) openly acknowledge and struggle with what I experienced, or (2) stuff it all in a box and hide it away in the furthest recesses of my mind and go forth as if it all neither happened nor existed. To put it in simpler terms, I could seek help and get better (i.e., become less dysregulated) or continue down the same path with no expectation that future results would look much different from past results.

This should have been an easy choice. And it was but not in the way you might expect. As Dr. McDonald has observed, "sometimes the stakes involved in integrating an experience are much higher than remaining dysregulated and locked in repeating patterns. Sometimes it's much easier to *repeat* a dynamic that it is to admit what is *behind* that dynamic." It's easier to pretend the monster doesn't exist than it is to acknowledge and confront the monster.

Not surprisingly, therefore, I chose to simply disregard, rather than confront, the monster, if for no other reason than it was, at the time, my only realistic option. I was unprepared (and unable) to confront what I had experienced and, quite frankly, did not really understand (or believe) that there was any way to help me deal with whatever it was that was destroying me from the inside. So, I just suppressed, or at least thought I suppressed, what I was feeling and returned to duty.

You're not flying the sanity kite very high either...so let's be crazy together.

Meg Collett, *The Killing Season*

My brief involuntary vacation provided a temporary respite from my internal struggles. Unfortunately, it provided no benefit to my relationship with Cynthia. The details of our collective dysfunction are not important. Cynthia and I, in different ways and for different reasons, badly needed partners on whom we could lean for support and assistance as we attempted to navigate a seemingly foreign world.

Unfortunately, neither of us possessed the skill set to provide the other what they needed. I was unable to provide Cynthia the stability and unconditional support she needed to help moderate the more extreme tendencies of her illness. Cynthia, likewise, was unable to provide the safety and security I needed to ease my dysregulation and distrust of the world.

Simply put, given our respective failings and shortcomings, each of us actually highlighted and exacerbated some of the other's worst tendencies and behaviors. There was nothing substantial about our relationship or anything that we did. We were not building anything worthwhile or making any real pretense at being or becoming adults. We were simply two souls hopelessly adrift, two quasi-adults attempting to navigate the emotional turmoil bombarding our brains and bodies.

Despite our never-far-from-the-surface dysfunction, Cynthia and I, at least on some level, actually had a lot of fun together. We spent far too much time watching off-the-beaten-path movies at a local independent theater. We also regularly attended showings of Rocky Horror Picture Show, generally participating in the crowd-based antics that make this unusual film even more enjoyable. We made fast friends with the staff of King Fong's, a Chinese restaurant in downtown Omaha which we frequented far too often. We even hung out with Mojo Nixon one night following a performance before a "crowd" of maybe 3 dozen people.

While we cared for each other in some sense of the word, neither of us was really capable of sacrificing for the other or for the greater good of our relationship. We were each more than willing to disregard the other to satisfy our individual needs or desires. Our respective shortcomings and difficulties, at times, almost demanded such behavior. So, naturally, we decided to get married shortly after I was discharged from the Air Force. It should come as no surprise that the marriage was short-lived.

The likelihood that our marriage would have been successful under any circumstances was pretty much zero. Moving to Michigan shortly after we were married, however, made divorce an inevitability. I only realized too late how detrimental it was for Cynthia to move away from her family and support system. As a result, the extremes of her illness became even more pronounced.

It is not uncommon for sufferers of bi-polar disorder to engage in incredibly dysfunctional and/or inappropriate behavior when in the grips of their illness. Some become promiscuous, others engage in physically reckless behavior, and still others engage in excessive shopping sprees. Fortunately (I think), Cynthia's go-to move was to shop, shop, and then shop some more. Cynthia loved clothes, the more fashionable the better. You might think that our lack of resources, would make it difficult for Cynthia to scratch this itch. Cynthia was not so easily deterred, however. She simply determined that if she could not legitimately purchase clothing, she would obtain it through various forms of theft and retail fraud.

Somewhere deep in the archives of the Ann Arbor police department and the Washtenaw County court system you can find the evidence of Cynthia's brief, yet quite ambitious, crime spree. While Cynthia's schemes and artifices were, for their day, creative, her eventual discovery was inevitable. My realization of Cynthia's crime spree, however, was much delayed. So much so that by the time I realized Cynthia's predicament, she was facing numerous charges of retail fraud for which some significant punishment could not be ruled out.

At that moment, it struck me that I had a decision to make. In my mind, Cynthia was flushing her life down the toilet and I had to decide if I wanted to go along for the ride. In a very real sense, it was not until these events that I truly understood what it would take for our marriage to have any chance of success. It wasn't that I hadn't before witnessed or bore the brunt of the extremes of Cynthia's illness. This circumstance, however, threatened me in a way that I had not previously experienced or perceived.

Because I am nothing if not a survivor, it was not difficult for me to make the decision to end our marriage. Moreover, there were no discussions, negotiations, or attempts at reconciliation. Instead, I contacted Cynthia's parents and informed them that their daughter would be arriving in Omaha via train a few days later. I then informed Cynthia that I was sending her back home. Her immediate response was, unfortunately, neither surprising nor, in a general sense, unfamiliar. Cynthia had long, gorgeous, flowing hair. Knowing that I found her tresses so appealing, Cynthia, determined to punish me, took my razor and carefully removed every hair on her head, forcing me to watch the entire process.

The manner in which I ended our marriage is not something of which I am proud. Cynthia certainly deserved better. Sending Cynthia back home to be with her parents was, however, without any doubt, best for both us. Nonetheless, that the result was appropriate does not diminish the embarrassment I felt (and still feel) about how that result was accomplished. Needless to say, once our marriage was over, *it was over*, and putting the entire episode completely behind me was much easier than I would have expected.

I have communicated with Cynthia only twice since putting her on the train back to Omaha. We spoke on the phone once as the details of our divorce were being resolved. Then, roughly 20 years later we stumbled across each other on Facebook. Mildly curious to learn how the other was doing, we sent a few messages back and forth. After discovering that we were both happy and doing reasonably well (or at least much better than when we were together), we terminated our exchange as we simply didn't have anything further to say to each other. It felt then, and still feels, as if my experience with Cynthia occurred in a different life and involved a different person. In a sense, that is not inaccurate. Ultimately, while my relationship with Cynthia was relatively brief, the experience would play a significant role later in my life.

The First Law of Holes: When you
Find Yourself in One, Stop Digging

Unknown

It was not immediately apparent, but sending Cynthia back to Nebraska was a significant turning point in my life. It was the point at which I began, at long last, to respect the First Law of Holes. Granted, I was not yet able to stop digging, but at least I slowly began to backfill into the immense hole in which I found myself more dirt than I was shoveling out. Not surprisingly, it was my grandparents who shepherded me through this transition with a significant assist from my brothers.

Following Cynthia's return home, I remained in Michigan to help care for my grandparents who were by this point in need of some assistance. My grandfather, nearing 80 years of age, was experiencing generally deteriorating health exacerbated by twice-weekly kidney dialysis. My grandmother, already north of 80, was in generally good health save her eyesight. By this time, macular degeneration had robbed my grandmother of much of her eyesight making it difficult for her to accomplish many ordinary tasks. They were still able, however, to live on their own with some assistance.

Nothing I helped them with was particularly difficult or challenging. For example, I took my grandmother shopping, shoveled the drive and mowed the lawn, helped transport my grandfather to and from dialysis, and assisted with a variety of tasks around the house. I lived and worked nearby, so I would often stop over for lunch or dinner (or both) and just hang out. This brief period with my grandparents was instrumental in my subsequent development.

It certainly helped that my grandparents were, albeit in different ways, incredible people. My grandmother was the most emotionally generous person I've ever experienced. She also exhibited an incredibly positive outlook on life, but she was hardly naïve having served for many years as a volunteer for Family Services and Children's Aid, a local social services agency. In this capacity, my grandmother witnessed myriad forms of familial dysfunction and the damage left in its wake. My grandmother seemingly understood that I was struggling with a great many things even if she was unaware of the specifics. In response, my grandmother showered me with kindness and patience.

While my grandmother blessed me with positive energy, my grandfather's gift was simply the power of his example. My grandfather was one of the smartest and most talented people I have ever known. He was a talented, self-taught, artist as well as a largely self-taught engineer. At the outbreak of World War II, he enlisted in the Army and served in Europe utilizing his skills as part of a mortar crew. Following the war, my grandfather worked as a design engineer for several organizations, most notably Adrian Steel whose commercial vehicle storage systems still embody many of his designs and innovations. In retirement, my grandfather designed and built a miniature Victorian house which was ultimately donated to a local museum.

Simply put, this period with my grandparents was an opportunity to receive, in the most general sense, some of the "parenting" I never received in my youth. While this was incredibly beneficial, it is important to try and understand at least part of the reason my grandparents' efforts were at least somewhat successful in (finally) pointing me in a positive direction.

First, while any sort of formal and/or professional therapy was still in the distant future, this period was nevertheless therapeutic. I was still not ready to confront what I had experienced and what was causing me to experience so much distress. Even if I had been willing to participate in some form of therapy or similar treatment, I doubt it would have proven particularly beneficial because of the extreme state of emotional dysregulation and distress I was still experiencing.

For therapy or similar treatment to be successful, you first have to trust the person with whom you are working. You must also be able to tap into your higher order functioning without getting unreasonably bogged down by emotional or instinctual lizard brain thinking. At this juncture, I was incapable of trusting anybody enough to share what I had experienced. Moreover, even if I had overcome this hurdle, I lacked the ability to explore what was ailing me without going all lizard brain. As strange as it may sound, I needed help before I could get help.

To be clear, I am *not* suggesting that you have to "get better" before seeking out professional assistance. What I am suggesting, however, is that there exist more avenues and resources to healing and growing than participation in therapy. Managing life's garbage is a journey over a variety of terrain and what (or who) can best help you get from point A to point B in your journey may not be what (or who) can best help you get from point B to point C.

As Dr. McDonald observes, "when we believe that the only place trauma healing can occur is in a therapist's office, we miss how very powerful and healing we all are for each other, all the time. Any relationship that can provide you with a relational home, a place where you can get help bearing what is unbearable, is a therapeutic one." Dr. McDonald relates how she came to realize this truth:

> I have worked extensively with two populations I have almost nothing in common with: combat veterans and previously incarcerated gang members. With members of both populations I acted in my capacity as a life coach who specialized in trauma and was there to help them reintegrate into society. Sometimes we talked about the future

but mostly about the present — the very present, the just-this-morning present. They would tell me about the way the present can get completely and suddenly eclipsed by the past. I would do all I could: I validated, demystified, and gave them tools. We would make plans and troubleshoot and check back in with tiny wins and big ole stumbles.

What I did not expect to hear as often as I did was this: "You get it, MC. You. Get. It.

Hearing those words always stunned me. On the face of it, I absolutely *do not* get it. I do not have any life experience that helps me understand what it is like to be born into a family of gang members and recruited into a gang at the age of seven. I do not have any life experience that helps me understand what it is like to be summarily dismissed from career military service because you are struggling with crippling anxiety after four tours in Iraq. I think what they were really saying was this: "You attune to me. We are allies. You stop here and stand with me in front of this overgrown garden. When I am feeling overwhelmed, you help me find where the weeds are. You stretch to help me pull them. We tend together, and we grow."

What I realized was that I don't have to have lived it to "get it." Shared experience is *not* what lays the foundation for a relational home. Attunement is. Which means that any of us can get better at knowing how to attune to someone. Any of us can learn to find which pieces of an experience are especially overwhelming. We can learn how to point out these pieces and ask, if we are able, whether we might hold them for a little while, like a colicky baby, so the other person can get a break.

What better place to get attunement, or unconditional acceptance, than your grandparents? My grandparents were, in a very real sense, my therapists for several years. Equally important is that as I began to stumble out of my personal wilderness, my internal perceptions of what was possible, while not wildly optimistic, were not entirely devoid of hope.

We're all familiar in some sense with people that seem to have a knack for consistently making "bad life choices" or who repeatedly gravitate towards unhealthy or abusive relationships. More than we perhaps realize, this is often driven by subconscious biology rather than conscious assessment. As Dr.

Perry has observed, "[t]he most destabilizing thing for anyone is to have their core beliefs challenged." Thus, "all of us tend to gravitate to the familiar, even when the familiar is unhealthy or destructive." Or, stated differently, "we feel better with the certainty of misery than the misery of uncertainty."

Given this knowledge, and in light of my upbringing, it might have seemed that I was practically destined to carry on my mother's legacy of bad life decisions and unhealthy relationships. This might very well have been my fate were it not for a few people who, in my youth, planted seeds in my subconsciousness that would later offer me hope that I need not follow in my mother's footsteps. While my time with these people was limited, their impact on me was profound.

My grandparents, not surprisingly, headline this group. They showed me that a home need not be enveloped in dysfunction and uncertainty and, moreover, that two individuals with wildly different interests and temperaments can have a successful marriage. They also embodied various traits that I have tried to emulate including intellectual curiosity, hard work and delayed gratification, and a belief in something larger than yourself.

While it's hardly breaking news that my grandparents had such a significant impact on me, it is less obvious perhaps that the other group from whose kindness in my youth I most benefitted was my brothers and their families. Their contribution to my later success is even more notable considering that given our collective circumstance it was not a given that we would have, following the end of their father's marriage to my mother, anything resembling a positive relationship.

The brief marriage between their father and my mother must have been incredibly difficult for my brothers. After losing their mother at such young ages, their father married a woman whose instability and unfitness as a parent only added to the distress they were already experiencing. That my mother ended their marriage leaving their father heartbroken seemingly only added insult to injury. Were I in their shoes, I'm not sure I would have been particularly eager to continue associating with a child of the woman who so thoroughly upended my life and family. Fortunately for me, my brothers are cut from different cloth.

While I didn't often see my brothers after our family split apart, they always made an effort to spend time with me whenever I visited Michigan to visit my grandparents. Our time together was spent doing pretty ordinary things, but similarly to the time spent with my grandparents my brothers demonstrated to me that it was possible to live without the endless chaos and dysfunction that characterized life with my mother. Likewise, they modeled various personal traits, such as hard work and ingenuity, integrity, and concern for others that I have strived to embody.

I realize it may be difficult to understand just how significant the time my grandparents and brothers spent with me in my youth turned out to be. It is not easy to articulate and my attempt seems lacking. Consider the situation a bit differently, however. How reasonable does it seem to expect a child to seek out (let alone attain) some version of life and themselves of which they have no knowledge or experience? Sounds to me like wishful (or delusional) thinking. It may sound harsh, but there was little to nothing about my experience living with my mother that could fairly be characterized as modeling or preparing me for the life I ultimately achieved. However, my grandparents and my brothers offered me a glimpse of what was possible. While it was not, through no fault of their own, enough to offset at the time what I was experiencing at home (and in my own head), without their efforts my life would almost certainly have ultimately ended up in a much darker and more dysfunctional place.

To be successful at anything, the truth is you don't have to be special. You just have to be what most people aren't – consistent, determined, and willing to work for it.

Tom Brady

After spending a few years with my grandparents, the ground beneath me began to feel slightly more stable and navigable. I was ready for something else. At the time, I was working as a Customer Service Representative for Manpower, a temporary employment agency. If you know anything about me and my temperament, you understand how utterly ill-suited I was for this position. I performed well enough to avoid termination, but it was a low-paying dead-end job that I was constitutionally incapable of performing long-term.

Unlike others who undoubtedly dreamt of becoming lawyers from an early age, the thought never crossed my mind. My long-standing interest in American history had introduced me to many interesting legal topics and events, however, becoming a lawyer was, in my mind, simply beyond my ability and station. One day, however, I recalled the lawyer who represented me in my divorce. Nice enough guy, but he was an idiot or at least idiot adjacent. Nevertheless, he was quite successful and it slowly dawned on me that if this guy could become a successful lawyer, why couldn't I do the same? So, I did.

Law school wasn't necessarily *fun*, but it was challenging. Moreover, it was the challenge I *needed.* Up to that point I had utterly failed to exert any real effort to develop or apply the skills I appeared to possess but had kept well hidden. While I was still very much a hot mess, I had at least progressed enough to (hopefully) take advantage of the opportunity law school presented. Just as I previously understood the personal cost should I fail to successfully adapt to military life, I understood that failure to succeed in law school had the very real potential to doom me to a lifetime of unsatisfying and depressing work. I wasn't particularly confident that I could pull it off but I figured if I just outworked everybody I at least had a puncher's chance.

Pushed and challenged to maximize my talent and ability for really the first time, I responded in a way I did not believe possible. Turned out, I was actually pretty good at this legal stuff and I graduated near the top of my class earning various honors and awards along the way. Of these, the most significant was probably the least publicized, a letter I received from Professor Wayne LaFave following first semester exams.

WAYNE R. LaFAVE
Professor Emeritus in the College of Law
and the Center for Advanced Study

College of Law
University of Illinois
504 E. Pennsylvania Avenue
Champaign, Illinois 61820
(217) 333-4268
FAX (217) 244-1478

December 22, 1995

Russell D. Ambrose
1839 Perrysville Road
Danville, IL 61832

Dear Russell:

As is my custom, I am writing to inform you that you received a grade of A in the Criminal Procedure course. Your numerical score placed you fourth in the class of 73 students. That is a very fine performance, and I commend you for it. I hope that you did as well in your other courses, and that you will continue to excel as you proceed with your legal education here at the University of Illinois.

Because in the past letters such as this one have often prompted an inquiry as to whether I would be a reference, I have now decided it is best for me to anticipate such questions by an affirmative indication up front. When that time comes, I would only ask that you drop a copy of your resume off with me. Again, congratulations on your excellent work in the criminal procedure course.

Yours sincerely,

The importance of this letter was two-fold. The first year of law school is like trying to drink water from a fire hose. Only the delusional or naturally gifted would suggest otherwise. Being neither, anxiety was the order of the day. Not surprisingly, my anxiety, which hovered around 11 on good days, began to spike even higher after the conclusion of first-semester exams. I just assumed, moreover, that my anxiety would continue to build until grades were announced several weeks later.

Because he wintered in Key West, Professor LaFave was motivated to quickly grade his exams. Thus, I received his letter very shortly after exams were concluded and before receiving my other grades. While receiving this letter did not completely eliminate my anxiety regarding my other grades, it did provide a much welcomed, and much needed, confidence boost. Professor LaFave's class was incredibly difficult and performing this well was the first indication that attending law school was the right choice.

This recognition was significant also because of the person with whom it was earned. I don't recall the circumstances, but I met Chuck LeFebvre in the first session or two of LaFave's class. Realizing our mutual interest in the subject matter, we immediately began studying together and hanging out. Chuck has been my best friend ever since. His friendship has been invaluable over the years in helping me grow and gain my footing both personally and professionally.

There is an observation about law school that the first year they scare you to death, the second year they work you to death, and the third year they bore you to death. There is a lot of truth in this observation and by the conclusion of law school I was certainly ready to move on. Fortunately, I exited law school with not just one job but two. Lest you think, however, that law school completely transformed me, upon graduation my classmates awarded me the following distinction:

Shortly after law school, I began working for the United States District Court for the Western District of Michigan serving as law clerk to Magistrate Judge Doyle A. Rowland. This was intended as a two-year adventure after which I would enter private practice with a local firm. Ultimately, however, private practice turned out to be the (very) temporary adventure after which I enjoyed a lengthy career with the court. My initial experience with the court, while enjoyable, ended on an unhappy note as Judge Rowland was killed in an automobile accident near the conclusion of my clerkship. I remained with the court until Ellen Carmody was selected as Judge Rowland's successor at which point I ventured off to Warner Norcross & Judd (WNJ).

In the movie *Interstellar*, Matthew McConnaughey bounces around the solar system desperately seeking planets hospitable for human life and habitation. On one of the planets he visits, every second that passes equals one day back on earth. After my brief tenure at WNJ, I have some appreciation for what it must feel like to explore the galaxy. While I was only with WNJ for a brief 8 months, it felt like a decade or longer. Warner Norcross & Judd is a tremendous law firm but private practice in a big-firm environment is just not a good fit for everybody. It certainly wasn't a good fit for me. So, when the opportunity arose to return to the court and serve as Judge Carmody's law clerk, I eagerly accepted.

For the next twenty-three plus years,[14] the court was my work home and provided an environment that enabled me to slowly get better and achieve personal growth I never imagined possible. How (and how much) working for the court benefitted me may not be immediately apparent. It seemingly wasn't apparent to those who worked most closely with me. For many years, I worked with Cynthia Hosner, Julie Lenon, and Judge Carmody during which time they consistently provided me an astounding level of support and encouragement which enabled me to (slowly) find my footing and eventually thrive.

While I shared with these women precious little about the baggage I was carrying around, or why it was so firmly strapped to my back, they all sensed that I was laboring under some significant burden.

---

[14] I served as Judge Carmody's law clerk for 18 years after which I began serving as law clerk to Magistrate Judge Phil Green.

Despite having a front row seat to my progress and growth, however, they have never really understood how (or how much) they helped me. For example, in response to my thanking her for everything she had done for me, Cynthia once responded, "but we didn't *do* anything." Claptrap.

Ultimately, the only person that can fix me, is me. While I have absolutely benefitted from many affirmative acts of assistance from a great many people, at the end of the day I'm the only one who can do the difficult work of self-improvement. Nevertheless, the environment and circumstances in which I undertake these efforts simply cannot be overlooked. Try growing tomatoes in a bed of nutrient deprived gravel and see what you end up with. It's no different with people. If you doubt this, just go back and re-read this work from the beginning. Environment and circumstances matter. Moreover, positive and nurturing environments, generally in short supply, do not happen by accident.

Part of the problem with being so dysregulated and life-skill deficient is that certain environments are simply not conducive to self-improvement and, in fact, can be counterproductive to such efforts. When I returned to the court, I still had very little understanding of what I was experiencing, or why. While I couldn't (or didn't want to) yet confront the monkey that was riding my back like a rented mule, I knew it was there and I knew I was the only one who could remove it. I didn't shy away from the effort, but I badly needed an environment that made success more likely. The environment that enveloped me every day I walked into the courthouse was absolutely the environment I needed. I realize this description is pretty vague, so let's try and put some meat on this bone.

As I noted earlier, quoting Dr. McDonald, "when we believe that the only place trauma healing can occur is in a therapist's office, we miss how very powerful and healing we all are for each other, all the time. Any relationship that can provide you with a relational home, a place where you can get help bearing what is unbearable, is a therapeutic one." In *The Boy Who Was Raised as a Dog*, Dr. Perry provides a moving example of this observation based on his work with the children who were rescued from the Branch Davidian compound near Waco, Texas.

The Mount Carmel religious community, more commonly known as the Branch Davidian compound, was led by David Koresh. Life for children in the compound was traumatic. The children suffered beatings, deprivation of food, and sexual assault. Koresh also instilled in his followers the fear that the "unbelievers" would eventually arrive at the compound to slaughter their entire community. To prepare for such, every member of the community, including children, were forced to participate in military training. They were also trained how to most effectively commit suicide should such become necessary when confronted by the "unbelievers."

In February 1993, agents with the Bureau of Alcohol, Tobacco and Firearms (BATF) approached the compound to arrest Koresh on weapons charges. To Koresh, this represented his prophecy come to life. The unbelievers had arrived to subjugate and kill him and his followers. Koresh refused to be taken into custody and the ensuing standoff resulted in the deaths of four BATF agents and at least six members of the Branch Davidians. The standoff continued for several days during which the FBI secured the release of twenty-one children. Dr. Perry led the team that began treating these children upon their rescue from the Branch Davidian compound.

Perry understood that "traumatized children. . .need predictability, routine, a sense of control and stable relationships with supportive people." Thus, while some of Perry's team wanted to immediately start conducting formal therapy with the children, Dr. Perry "felt it was more important [to first] restore order and be available to support, interact with, nurture, respect, listen to, play with, and generally 'be present.'" As Dr. Perry described:

> I thought these children needed the opportunity to process what had happened at their own pace and in their own ways. If they wanted to talk, they could come to a staff member that they felt comfortable with; if not, they could play safely and develop new childhood memories and experiences to begin offsetting their earlier fearful ones. We wanted to offer structure, but

not rigidity; nurturance, but not forced affection.

Each night after the children went to bed our team would meet to review the day and discuss each child. This "staffing" process began to reveal patterns that suggested therapeutic experiences were taking place in short, minutes-long interactions. As we charted these contacts we found that, despite having no formal "therapy" sessions, each child was actually getting hours of intimate, nurturing, therapeutic connections each day. The child controlled when, with whom, and how she interacted with the child-sensitive adults around her. Because our staff had a variety of strengths – some were very touchy-feely and nurturing, others were humorous, still others good listeners or sources of information – the children could seek out what they needed, when they needed it. This created a powerful therapeutic web.

While I was allegedly an adult and not newly rescued from the clutches of a deadly cult, I was in a general sense in the same circumstance as those children – struggling with the aftermath of unresolved traumatic events. If anything, the fact that the events causing me so much difficulty were, temporally speaking at least, so far in the past made my circumstance even more challenging.

The description by Dr. Perry immediately above is an incredibly accurate description of what I experienced every day I walked into the courthouse. Serving as a law clerk is, for the most part, a relatively isolated position with a significant degree of autonomy. While I enjoyed the autonomy and isolation of my job, I spent a great deal of time engaging and interacting with the folks in our office and within the rest of the court. Importantly, however, I was largely able to control when such interactions occurred and these interactions were, to varying degrees, incredibly therapeutic.

In short, I was surrounded by caring people who, even if they knew nothing of what I was struggling with, desired an environment in which somebody like me could thrive, and they did the things both large and small to make that a reality. My friends and co-workers didn't do this *for me* (although I'm confident they would have if asked), they did it because it's simply who they are. Thus, my friends and co-workers may not have *done* anything for me, at least in the sense Cynthia meant it, nonetheless they gave me everything. And I am eternally grateful.

Come live your life with me. Only thing
I ask is that you outlive me so I never
have to live another day without you.

Beth Dutton, *Yellowstone*

As spectacularly as my first marriage failed, I hit the
matrimonial jackpot the second time around.

Second only to my grandmother, Lisa is the kindest
and most giving person I have ever known. For more
than 25 years our relationship has provided me
something that largely eluded me growing up – a
home where I felt physically and emotionally safe.
Having such a refuge has enabled me to slowly find
my footing in life and grow and develop into the
person I have since become.

Lisa and I are incredibly compatible in many important respects. We are both honest and hard-working. Our basic values and interests generally align. We respect each other and enjoy each other's company. While these are all important aspects of a relationship, it is our compatibility on a more fundamental level that underlies the success of our marriage.

I'm not really sure if I have a personal credo, but if I do it is represented by the following poster which is displayed prominently in my workshop:

LONELINESS
is unrecognized serenity

From an early age, I learned to isolate and retreat within. Solitude feels so much more natural to me than any other state and is, absent some positive force or encouragement, my default state. As you can probably imagine, there are probably not many successful e-Harmony profiles for "cranky hermit seeks randomly intermittent (at best) female companionship." Moreover, it's not just that I tend toward isolation. Instinctually, my default is to actively push away anybody who tries to get too close. Simply put, trying to get close to me can be like trying to hug a cactus. . .and the closer you get, the sharper the spines become.

While Lisa, fortunately, does not share my general aversion to people or social interaction, getting close to her is no less daunting a task. Lisa and I are, to put it simply, two of the most guarded and emotionally independent people you could ever meet. We're like fugu, a type of poisonous puffer fish. If handled properly, fugu is considered an incredible delicacy. If handled improperly, however, fugu will make for a very bad day. Just as there are not many people who know how to properly handle fugu, there aren't many people who truly understand what makes us tick and with whom we would be compatible.

Fortunately, we each sensed, on slightly differing timelines, our fundamental compatibility. Lisa realized relatively quickly that I had no desire to control her or limit what she could do or accomplish. Took me a bit longer, but I eventually realized that not only was I safe with Lisa but that she would actually work and sacrifice for my benefit. We were fortunate to discover each other. However, having stumbled across the person with whom I *could* make an incredible life was no guarantee that such would occur. Here is where the lessons learned from my first attempt at marriage proved valuable.

While my first marriage was, by any definition, unsuccessful, there were lessons to be discovered in the wreckage. The question was whether I could discover them and, more importantly, whether I would heed them. I would never claim the ability to fully discern the lessons or insights to be gleaned from any personal relationship or interaction. However, were it not for the insights gained from my first marriage, it's unlikely my marriage to Lisa would have survived or been so successful.

The first lesson I learned was "eat your vegetables." As I noted previously, my relationship with Cynthia was incredibly superficial. Our marriage didn't fail because of a lack of compatibility. Cynthia and I appeared in many respects to be quite "compatible." However, we simply lacked the ability (or interest) to do the hard work necessary to make a relationship work. I was determined not to make the same mistake again. In simple terms, I understood that for any second marriage to be successful, I needed to be more willing to do some of the heavy lifting necessary for a relationship to succeed. Likewise, I needed a partner just as willing to help in this regard. In this regard, I could not have hoped for a better partner. Don't get me wrong, neither of us are opposed to dessert. We have just come to understand that the fun and less serious aspects of being together are even more enjoyable and meaningful because our marriage rests upon a solid foundation of vegetables.

The other big lesson I learned from my first marriage was that some vegetables taste better than others. News flash – marriage is hard. It's hard enough for two reasonably well-adjusted people with minimal baggage (assuming any such people exist). It can occasionally become more difficult, however, when one or both partners are carrying around more than their fair share of emotional or personal baggage. One of the things that strengthens our relationship is we each have a visceral understanding of the difficulties the other has experienced. Not surprisingly, however, sometimes our individual shortcomings or blind spots have made constructing a strong marriage a little more difficult.

A few years into our marriage, we (or at least I) hit a pretty rough stretch. Granted, the difficulties we were experiencing, while not insignificant, were not in the same neighborhood as the kinds of difficulties that reasonably or justifiably cause marriages to fail. Nevertheless, I very seriously contemplated divorce. It was a struggle. I felt as if I was attempting to traverse landscape that was difficult and unfamiliar yet, simultaneously, all too familiar. Ultimately, it was this familiarity, rather than a fear of the unknown, that tipped the scales. I could stomach a lot of things but becoming my mother and mimicking her history of failed marriages was not one of them. I *knew* I had picked the right life partner, I just needed to (re)commit to making things work. In short, I needed to eat a few more vegetables even some that, at the time, I found less than pleasant.

I've little doubt that Lisa has experienced more than her share of similar (or worse) frustrations or difficulties. I can only imagine how difficult it must be at times to be married to me. A wannabe hermit clothed in practically impenetrable armor is a hard nut to crack. Fortunately, she has never attacked or attempted to breach my armor as others have. Instead, she has supported me and enriched my life to such a degree that while I'm not yet able to completely discard my armor, I am able to set it aside with increasing frequency. Because of Lisa, I am a much better person and partner.

Not all storms come to disrupt your life.
Some come to clear your path.

Unknown

Over the years, I've often mused that at some point as we age "shit starts breaking or falling off." Indeed. I recently learned that I have retinitis pigmentosa (RP), a rare disease which causes the retina to deteriorate, resulting in a variety of vision difficulties and, ultimately, blindness.

Technically, RP is not a single disease but rather a term used to identify a group of similar eye diseases all of which affect the retina. The retina, which rests in the rear of your eye, is central to your ability to experience vision. Think of your retina as housing thousands of tiny individual cameras which capture light and transmit it through your optic nerve to your brain enabling you to "see" the world. My retinas are failing as these scans/images (performed December 2023) reveal.

Right eye (OD) / **12/12/2023 / 10:05:59**
Grayscale (VA)

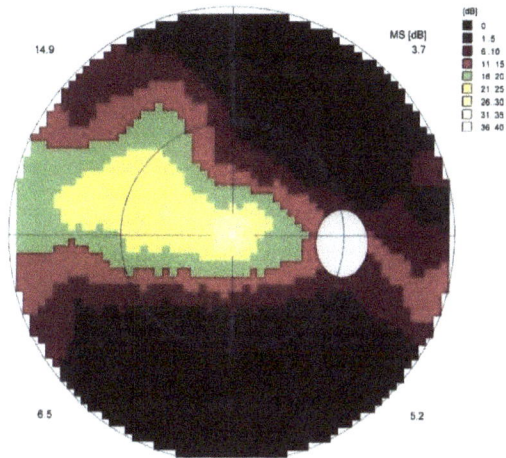

MS [dB]
3.7

[dB]	
	0
	1 5
	6 10
	11 15
	16 20
	21 25
	26 30
	31 35
	36 40

14.9

6 5

5.2

Left eye (OS) / **12/12/2023 / 10:12:56**
Grayscale (VA)

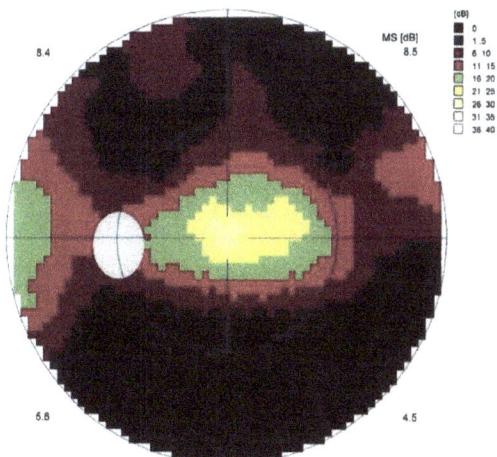

MS [dB]
8.5

[dB]	
	0
	1 5
	6 10
	11 15
	16 20
	21 25
	26 30
	31 35
	36 40

8.4

5.8

4.5

The black areas represent portions of my retinas that have effectively died. At the other extreme, the yellow and green areas represent relatively healthy areas of my retinas. The "reddish" areas lie somewhere between these two extremes. One thing that is apparent from these images, and which I can confirm through experience, is that significant portions of my retinas simply don't function. In other words, most of the tiny cameras in my retinas are either completely non-functional or significantly impaired. I can still "see," but my vision is inconsistent, not entirely reliable, and subject to various types of "noise" and interference. Moreover, my field of vision is shrinking.

It is easy to think of sight as a binary concept – in other words, you either can see or you can't. It is more accurate, however, to consider sight as existing on a continuum. In his wonderful book, *The Country of the Blind: A Memoir at the End of Sight*, Andrew Leland notes that only a small percentage (roughly 15 percent) of legally blind people have no light perception. The vast majority of "blind" people have some degree of light perception but are nonetheless unable to "see" due to other complications or failings with their eyes and/or visual network. While I am certainly not (yet) legally blind, I am nevertheless moving along the continuum away from healthy sight.

In addition to experiencing all-too-frequent instances of "visual noise" or "visual miscalibration," my visual acuity appears to be somewhat of a moving target varying throughout the day in sometimes subtle, but nonetheless irritating, ways. My relationship with light is also increasingly problematic, but the circumstance is more nuanced than simply bright light "bad" and dim light "good." Certainly, my threshold for what constitutes too bright or too dim has changed significantly. However, more than simply experiencing a diminished range of acceptable light intensity, the source or location of light is usually a greater source of irritation or difficulty than the intensity thereof. Also, transitions from one level of light intensity to another (e.g., from bright light to shadow or vice versa) present significant difficulty. For example, riding along a tree-lined country road on a sunny day is an exercise in frustration. As the car rapidly transitions from sun-to-shade-to-sun, ad nauseum, my vision practically shuts down because it can no longer process such rapidly changing lighting conditions. However, two of the most significant ways in which my vision is deteriorating relate to the blind spots in my retinas and the diminishment of my field of vision.

Regarding the former, the blind spots in my retinas have advanced to the point that it is not uncommon for me to momentarily not see objects right in front of me. To understand this phenomenon, it is important to understand that what we experience as "vision" is far more complicated than we realize. Neuroscientists have learned that "our brains do not rely solely on what is shown to the eyes in order to 'see.' Instead the brain constructs a complex prediction."[15]   Research and experimentation reveals that "[e]ffectively, our brains construct an incredibly complex jigsaw puzzle using any pieces it can get access to. These are provided by the context in which we see them, our memories and our other senses." Simply put, "[t]he brain's main function is to minimize surprise – that is what it has evolved to do."

Likewise, Peter Gärdenfors, Ph.D. observes that "[w]hat you experience is not the world itself. . .but your brain's construction of it. . .Nature itself is colorless, soundless, and scentless; it's just matter moving around meaninglessly. Our senses give it content. The brain is therefore not a passive recipient of images and sounds from the world around us. It actively looks for patterns and interprets the world around it."[16] While her work extends well beyond sight and vision issues, neuroscientist Chantel Prat, Ph.D., in *The Neuroscience of You*, offers insight into how this predictive process works:

---

[15] *What Our Eyes Can't See, the Brain Fills In*, University of Glasgow, April 5, 2011. (https://www.gla.ac.uk/news/archiveofnews/2011/ap ril/headline_194655_en.html).

[16] *How the Brain Fills in the Blanks*, Psychology Today, December 7, 2023 (https://www.psychologytoday.com/us/blog/what-is-a-human/202312/how-the-brain-fills-in-the-blanks).

One of the most essential ways your experiences shape your brain is through a process called Hebbian learning. In essence, Hebbian learning is the biological mechanism that allows your brain to keep a running set of statistics about how frequently things occur in your environment. Much like sports teams keep statistics of their players and use them to make decisions about who to start and who to trade, your brain has a way of "counting" the frequency of occurrences of different types of events and using this system to figure out what's most likely to be happening, given the incomplete information it receives.

Fortunately, your brain's way of taking statistics doesn't require any counting on your part. Instead, the work happens in the connections between the gossipy neurons - in the spaces that determine who is talking to whom, and how loudly. Timing is really important for organizing such communication. As it turns out, it's also really important for learning. When two neurons in close proximity become excited at approximately the same time, the connections between them will strengthen, increasing the likelihood that the message of one will be picked up by the other. Though the actual principles of Hebbian learning are a bit more nuanced than this, I always remembered the catchy slogan I first learned as an undergrad: "Neurons that fire together, wire together." And the more often this happens, the stronger the connection between the two neurons will grow. This is your brain's way of connecting the dots. It assumes that if events A and B virtually always occur at the same time, they are part of the same "neural event." Once this happens, even if your brain only gets evidence that A is going on in the outside world, it is likely to assume that B happened as well, and will *create* that experience for you.

There are other examples which illustrate the complexity underlying what we "see." For example, several years ago the world was captivated by a picture of a dress which to some people appeared white and gold but appeared blue and black to others. This discrepancy was caused by the fact that the photograph provided very little context regarding the nature of the light which was striking the dress. As Dr. Prat explains:

> Under this circumstance, people's brains make different assumptions automatically about what the light is like in the picture. Those of you that see a white and gold dress do so because your brain assumes, based on

your lifetime of experiences with light sources, that light is coming from behind and that the dress is in a shadow. To fix this it automatically subtracts out the dark blue and black hues and leaves you seeing white and gold. Others, like me, who see the dress as blue and black, assume that it is well lit from the front or top, possibly through some source of artificial lighting and so we make no such subtraction.

My brain generally does a good job compensating for the blind spots in my vision by "filling in the blanks" and presenting me with an accurate depiction of the world. Sometimes, however, my brain, lacking sufficient visual input and/or relational data to compensate for the blind spots in my retinas, simply communicates to me an incomplete picture of the world. Thus, I often simply fail to see items that are literally right in front of me. Likewise, I occasionally knock over or bump into items because I am simply unaware of their presence. This failure to "see" something is usually fleeting. Once a moment passes and I move my head or otherwise re-orient myself relative to an object, my brain, having received more and/or different input will then provide me with a more accurate or more complete view of the world. Still, it is difficult to describe how disconcerting and irritating this experience is. However, it is something with which I am coming to terms because as my retinas continue to deteriorate it is something I am more frequently experiencing.

A couple anecdotal examples may help illustrate what I'm experiencing. The first involves our dogs and represents the moment I realized I could no longer drive. We have a large field with mowed paths on which we take our dogs for walks. They wander around off-leash, remaining relatively close but free to run around living their best dog life. When the dogs are walking in front of me and I turn away for a moment, I experience no difficulty seeing the dogs when I turn my head back in their direction. My brain, having identified the dogs' location only a moment earlier, is able to pair that information with whatever visual input my eyes provide, as well as any other relevant input such as the dogs barking, and quickly communicate the dogs' location.

One day while I was out with the dogs, they stopped to investigate something that caught their attention. Knowing the dogs would remain nearby, I simply walked past them and continued down the path. When I turned around, however, 10-15 seconds later, I could not spot the dogs. Unlike the circumstance above in which the dogs were walking in front of me, this time my brain did not possess the same quality or quantity of historical or relational information to compensate for my diminished visual input. As a result, when I turned around I was unable to visually locate the dogs. Then, a few seconds later, by which point my brain had accumulated additional input/information, the dogs simply appeared in my vision, 30 or so feet away coming up the path toward me.

Any thought that my dogs simply possessed the ability to shape-shift or become invisible was put to rest after experiencing the same general phenomenon multiple times in other circumstances and environments. For example, one day I visited a coffee shop with a friend who referenced a tip jar that was allegedly sitting on the counter. Tip jar? What tip jar? I didn't see any tip jar. . .until, of course, the tip jar appeared in my vision sitting on the counter easily within arm's reach. Having no previous experience with the interior of that coffee shop, my brain was forced to rely to a much greater extent on the visual input provided by my eyes to determine what was there. For whatever reason, due to the relative deficiency in data and visual input, my brain was unable for several seconds to realize that there was, in fact, a tip jar sitting on the counter in front of me.

This is the best explanation I can provide for something which is, in a sense, simply inexplicable. I've just accepted that my vision is apparently going out with a whimper rather than a bang and this is one of the ways in which my vision is whimpering into the night.

Diminished field of vision, another classic symptom of RP, is another way in which my vision is deteriorating. An easy way perhaps to understand this phenomenon, and how my RP is progressing, is to put on a hooded sweatshirt and pull the hood up over your head. If you pull the hood far enough up over your head, your field of vision will be restricted. You can still see, but your field of vision is limited. As you pull the strings of your sweatshirt tighter, your field of vision will get smaller and smaller until eventually you are left with a tiny pinhole of light. Pull the strings a little tighter still and all light is extinguished. In a general sense, that's how RP progresses. This is generally what I am experiencing although I am presently experiencing a greater loss in the upper and lower portions of my field of vision as opposed to my left and right peripheral vision. This can make navigating crowds or spaces with unfamiliar or uncertain terrain challenging because it is difficult for me to simultaneously see where I'm walking while seeing what is in front of me. Thus, I have taken to using a white cane when traveling alone.[17]

---

[17] My use of a white cane suggests that my vision is much worse than it actually is. As I explained to a man on a train, I was using the white cane as much for him as for me. There exists a very real possibility that when navigating unfamiliar spaces I will stumble and/or fall simply due to the restriction in my field of vision. If this occurs in public I'm likely to bump or fall into somebody and possibly injure them (or me) and/or damage their (or my) belongings. Rather than shoulder that risk (and embarrassment) I just deploy my cane, transforming into a modern-day Moses parting the sea of travelers allowing me to more easily move alone through unfamiliar spaces.

It is difficult to articulate what I'm experiencing regarding my vision. While I experience a variety of vision difficulties and limitations, I am able to "see" and, driving a car excepted, can still do the same things I have always done albeit often more slowly and deliberately. Presently, my biggest challenge is less an "absence of vision" and more a notable diminution in my ability to rely on "muscle memory" to navigate and interact with the world.

Navigating the world and using or manipulating common objects are activities which most of us simply take for granted. We simply accomplish these movements without much (if any) consideration whether our visual input is accurate. I can no longer take such things for granted, however. Instead, I must actively consider my movements because I commonly either fail to see all that is before me and/or cannot trust that what I visually perceive is an accurate depiction of the world. Because this is such a foreign concept, I often knock into or stumble over things because I either do not see something or misperceive its location in space.

When I was first diagnosed with RP, a retinal specialist told me that the practical question with my disease would be how quickly it progressed from "a pain in the ass" to "true disability." Fortunately, my circumstance is not yet disabling and may not reach that stage for a few years and perhaps not all at all. Still, it is a very large pain in the ass that is becoming more challenging to navigate.

Like most things in life, however, this circumstance is ultimately what I make of it. While the downside of my circumstance may be obvious, it is hardly doom and gloom. First, blindness or significant visual impairment is obviously not a death sentence. Moreover, while the loss of my vision will certainly make various tasks and activities more challenging, the paths to overcoming such are not unknown. Also, technological advances are making activities easier and more accessible for the visually impaired. Moreover, there exists a possibility that I might not ever completely lose my sight.

Because the diseases under the RP banner are all inherited, I participated in genetic testing to determine which RP genetic marker(s) I possessed. The good news is that the gene alteration responsible for my vision difficulties is associated with forms of RP that are sometimes more slowly advancing. Nobody knows or can predict how quickly or slowly my vision will decline. As I continue to undergo testing and examination, the accumulation of data may afford more informed speculation, but at this point trying to determine when (or even if) I'll become "blind" is merely speculation. Nevertheless, considering the results of testing thus far, as well as my day-to-day experience, the informed speculation at this point is that I probably have another 5-7 years of "functional vision."

While I would never characterize losing my vision as a good thing, there may be a bit of a silver lining to my circumstance. Those of us of a certain age grew up with *M*A*S*H*, a long-running television program which, in addition to the ever-present comedy, regularly explored more serious topics and themes. There is an episode in which Aggie, a war correspondent, becomes enamored with B.J. who then struggles to remain faithful to his wife back home. As the pair discuss their predicament, B.J. says, "Ag, you know what they say here? 'Live for now, for there may be no tomorrow.' There's a lot to be said for that. Not for me. I've got to live for tomorrow, because for me there's no now."

While B.J.'s comment concerns a very different circumstance, the sentiment nonetheless resonates. I have spent far too much of my life simply trying, in some sense, to simply survive from day-to-day propelled forward by a vague hope that someday in the "future" I would somehow transition from surviving to living. I've spent much of my life living for an imagined tomorrow because of an inability to find much real or meaningful enjoyment in the present.

One of the ways in which PTSD manifests is a limited ability to be "present." As Dr. McDonald observes:

> When your stress response system is in overdrive all the time, it becomes really easy to clue in to all the potential ways the world is dangerous and completely miss what is going on in the present moment. We become fixated on the infinite vulnerabilities and dwell on

potential loss, potential pain, and potential horror. That terror robs us of our present by mashing together problems from our past and our fears for the future. . .When hypervigilance becomes a way of life, all you see is potential threat – nothing else. Being in any kind of relationship with someone who is driven by that kind of fear is like trying to have a deep and vulnerable conversation with a sniper on watch. You can sit there and bare your soul as much as you like, but 99 percent of his focus is in the crosshairs.

This description certainly rings true with much of my experience although I would articulate it a bit more directly. After experiencing life as prey, you expend an incredible amount of physical and emotional energy assessing the world for threats which diminishes your ability to simply enjoy the present. Fortunately, as I have described throughout, my perception of the world as hostile and threatening has diminished notably. As I have become less dysregulated and more content, my ability to enjoy the present has increased. Nonetheless, my work in this regard is hardly complete.

Gradually losing my vision doesn't even make the top-10 of worse things I've experienced. Nevertheless, because sight is so central to our existence, and because of my somewhat advanced age, my RP diagnosis has produced an urgency (and anxiety) to learn to better enjoy life in the moment. It is easy to overdramatize my circumstance. We all have or will experience medical setbacks, many far worse than what I'm experiencing. Nevertheless, the experience of losing my sight has been a shock to the system that has prompted some modest, but not insignificant, life changes.

For example, I have decided to retire several years earlier than anticipated. This change is partly out of necessity as my eyesight makes it difficult for me to perform visually-taxing activities, such as reading and writing, for sustained periods of time. However, this decision is also driven by a desire to try and enjoy life a bit more. I plan to spend a great deal of time in my shop as woodworking will likely be the activity I am first compelled, once my vision deteriorates to a certain point, to give up or dramatically scale back. Fortunately, woodworking is not my only interest. I love to cook and am a reasonably skilled amateur. No better way to expand my skills (and enjoyment) than with some new gear and better designed space. So, our kitchen is presently undergoing a significant makeover.

As you might imagine, experiencing life from an extremely defensive posture is not particularly conducive to traveling or taking vacations. I am certainly not opposed to traveling and have been on several incredible vacations to various places across the country. It is, however, very difficult for me to overcome the inertia of remaining tethered to one of the most valuable things I now have but lacked for far too much of my life – a home where I feel safe and comfortable. Hoping that it will make overcoming my inertia a bit easier, we recently purchased a small camper. The early returns are promising as we have already utilized the camper on several occasions in the several months since its purchase. Finally, in perhaps my most ambitious or optimistic endeavor, I've taken up the piano at age 60. I've no idea what will come of this effort but it's always something I wanted to learn to do.

While I should have long ago confronted the detritus roaming around inside my head and learned to better enjoy and more fully experience life, I still have plenty of life ahead of me and look forward to enjoying these and other activities for as long as I'm able. The lesson here should be apparent, however. Don't wait for some imagined tomorrow to begin enjoying today. If there are obstacles in your path to achieving this goal, find the help you need to navigate the waters in which you find yourself. Don't struggle or live a diminished life for years on end like I have done. You deserve better.

> True peace is not for the spineless or self-absorbed. It has nothing to do with passivity or resignation. Peace demands honesty. It entails the burden of duty. Peace requires deeds of love.

Johann Christoph Arnold, *Seeking Peace*

It is appropriate that my parents, in a sense, serve as bookends to this work. My mother, integral in my early years, is central to the initial portions of this work. My father, on the other hand, was largely absent from my life until the end of his own life. Thus, it seems appropriate that he make an appearance toward the conclusion of this work.

In very different ways, I have felt the impact of my parents' shortcomings. While an oversimplification, if my mother's failings were errors of commission, my father's shortcomings were errors of omission. To understand the basis for this observation, we must return to my early childhood.

As already noted, my parents divorced when I was very young. A few years later my father moved overseas where he lived and worked for roughly the next 25 years. Thus, during my youth and teenage years, when I was experiencing many of the events that would cause me so much turmoil, my father was absent, literally and figuratively.

Because my father and his wife both worked in education, they always had several weeks off every summer and during the Christmas holiday. Not surprisingly, they travelled extensively during their breaks from school. As part of their travels, they returned to the U.S. every summer for several weeks to visit their parents, who lived in Michigan and Indiana, as well as friends in Michigan and various other locations across the country.

The one location to which my father could never be bothered to travel, however, was wherever I happened to be living at the time.[18] Growing up, if I wanted to spend time with my father, I had to travel to Michigan. This was less of an issue than would otherwise have been the case because I would have traveled to Michigan regardless to spend time with my grandparents and brothers. However, even when I travelled to Michigan my father rarely had much time for me (or even his own parents).

While my father's behavior caused me, at the time, to experience a great deal of hurt and anger, I eventually came to terms with the situation and accepted that my father was simply unwilling to forego his personal interests and desires for anybody else, including me. What was much harder to accept, however, was my father's subsequent

---

[18] I certainly recognize that non-custodial parents often experience difficulty trying to visit their children or otherwise remain involved in their life. Such was not the case in my circumstance, however. My mother, as disappointed with my father as I was, always made clear that my father was welcome to visit me any time.

inability and/or unwillingness to understand or accept any responsibility for his failures as a father.

One of the difficulties non-custodial parents often experience is finding themselves somewhat in the dark regarding the everyday events and circumstances of their child's life. Thus, I understand that my father may not have been expected to know what my life was like on a day-to-day basis. My father's failure was not that he was unable to observe what I was experiencing literally half a world away. Rather, his failure was in making no attempt to ensure that I was safe, despite having sufficient reason to investigate my living situation and well-being.

My father certainly knew how erratic and unstable my mother could be – that's why they so quickly divorced after my birth. Moreover, if my father ever harbored any doubt regarding my mother's instability and fitness as a parent, any such doubt should have vanished after my mother embarked on marriage number three which only occurred after my mother demonstrated an inability to settle down in one location for any appreciable length of time.

I would be beyond embarrassed if I fathered a child and then failed to take any affirmative steps to ensure that my child was safe and reasonably cared for. My embarrassment in this regard would increase exponentially if the woman with whom I had fathered a child was as erratic and unstable as my mother. It should be obvious that a child in such a circumstance would likely experience some kind of harm or deprivation. Thus, to do absolutely nothing in the face of such, as my father did, is simply the definition of parental irresponsibility.

Even had my father attempted to learn about my living situation such was no guarantee that he would have observed or learned about any of the various difficulties I was experiencing. He could have at least made an effort, however. He could have visited occasionally and observed where and how I was living. As an educator, he should have understood that reaching out to my teachers or other school officials might have shed light on my well-being.

I recognize that I could have at any time just told my father some of the things I was experiencing, but why would I share such things with somebody who seemed to care so little about me? More importantly, why was it incumbent upon me, the child, to assume the role of an adult for a man who wanted to act like a child? Had my father just made some minimal effort to demonstrate that he cared how I was doing, perhaps I would have felt differently.

There is not, to my knowledge, a statute of limitations on being a parent. Thus, even though my father made no effort, while I was young, to learn what I experienced, he could still have inquired about such after I reached adulthood. Understanding that once I reached adulthood, there was likely little impetus on my father's part to actively inquire about my childhood, I introduced the subject on two separate occasions, expressly inviting him to learn what my life was like growing up in the hope that he might engage in some much needed self-reflection.

Specifically, on two separate occasions, while discussing personal matters generally, I expressly stated that things for me, growing up and living with my mother, were a lot worse than he could possibly have realized. I phrased it in exactly those terms. Two things about these conversations are important to note. First, both conversations occurred when I was in my late 30s and, therefore, occurred well after my hospitalization discussed previously. Second, my father had first-hand knowledge that I had been hospitalized.

When I was hospitalized, one of the staff psychiatrists spoke with my father (with my permission). While I don't recall specifically what the psychiatrist shared with my father, he was informed that I had been involuntarily admitted to a psychiatric hospital for treatment. Despite undoubtedly understanding that people don't generally get whisked away on involuntary "vacations" because they are winning at life, my father *never* acknowledged or asked about my hospitalization and *never* expressed concern or interest in learning what led to my hospitalization.

Nevertheless, in an attempt to have some sort of conversation about the matter, I twice expressly invited my father to engage with the topic. In response to hearing that my life growing up was more difficult than he realized, the most my dad could muster was, "well, if I had known, I would have done something." The lack of self-awareness inherent in this response is simply staggering and represented, in my mind, a complete abdication of his role as parent.

As much as I wanted to ask my father if he understood that it was always easily within his power to know whether I was safe and adequately cared for as a child, I recognized the futility of such. My father was simply unwilling and/or incapable of discussing such matters or accepting any responsibility for his failure as a parent. So, I simply made my peace, as best I could, with the circumstance and moved on. My decision was aided by the realization that even if my father had obtained custody of me when I was young, such guaranteed nothing as it is simply impossible to know whether the path not taken would have resulted in a better or more satisfying life.[19]

Despite this impasse of sorts, my dad and I eventually began to communicate more and spend

---

[19] The wisdom inherent in this realization became even more apparent much later in life upon learning of the likely cause of the degenerative neurological disease from which my father and his wife died. According to my father's neurologists, the disease in question (discussed below) was very likely precipitated by exposure to pesticides. This assessment seems apt considering that my father and his wife lived in the developing world (e.g., Egypt, Zambia, Sri Lanka, Bangladesh, and Vietnam) for many years.

time together occasionally. From my perspective, however, there remained between us a barrier that prevented us from becoming close. Beggars can't be choosers, I suppose. Still, it was a surprise when, shortly after beginning this project, my father asked to move in with me and Lisa.

My father's request was prompted by the decline in health he was beginning to experience and the expectation that his health would continue to deteriorate significantly. My father was suffering from Progressive Supranuclear Palsy (PSP), the same disease which claimed his wife several years prior. PSP, often mistaken for Parkinson's Disease, is a rare neurological disease which attacks the parts of the brain controlling activities such as walking, balancing, and general movement. Considering that my father's health was rapidly declining, his inability to continue living alone was not a surprise. We just never expected that my father would ask to live with us.

While my father's request was unexpected, Lisa and I immediately agreed. My father's condition was deteriorating, it turns out even more quickly than we then anticipated, and despite the difficulty between us my father didn't deserve to die in a facility. Moreover, I would have done this for my father if for no other reason than it is what my grandmother would have wanted me to do.

I suspect that trepidation and uncertainty is normal whenever an aging parent moves in with an adult child. We certainly harbored concerns, especially considering my father's personality and many idiosyncrasies. In short, we expected my father's incorporation into our lives would present a challenge and this was before accounting for the increasing amount of assistance my father was going to require with basic daily functions. Our concerns, it turned out, were well-founded.

As my father's health and ability to function deteriorated, he required much more assistance than anticipated with even the most basic daily functions. Also, because it was difficult for him to accept what he was experiencing, my father was reluctant to allow us to obtain assistance to help us care for him. To compound matters, my father often made demands on us with respect to his care that ranged from merely irritating to utterly unreasonable. Nevertheless, understanding that his time was rapidly diminishing, we did our best to accommodate his needs and requests to hopefully maximize his rapidly diminishing quality of life.

There is no question that the hand my father was dealt at the conclusion of his life sucked. PSP is a nasty disease and having watched his wife be attacked by the same disease a few years earlier, my father *knew* how his disease would progress and, ultimately, how his life would end. Were I facing such a prospect, I can only imagine how sour my attitude would become. Nonetheless, we often wondered why my father wanted to come live out his days with us. Seemed a bit rude to just come out and ask, "why did you want to come live here?" Through less direct conversation, however, I learned that my father apparently desired some sort of rapprochement with me.

In light of my father's refusal, noted above, to engage in any sort of discussion regarding the challenges of my early life, his interest in trying to make amends with me was puzzling. Moreover, after my father moved in with us he did not seem to act like he desired bridging the gap that existed between us. He never indicated a desire to communicate with me about anything personal or substantial. Moreover, he refused to ever turn off the television and would often turn the volume up so as to prevent conversation. I would come to realize, however, that the difficulty with my father was not so much a lack of interest in making amends with me but instead a complete inability to do so.

While my father was unable to speak with me about our relationship, he was willing to address the matter with one of the nurses who helped care for him. Not surprisingly, I would subsequently learn that these conversations were initiated and undertaken largely at the nurse's encouragement. Sensing from their conversations that my dad was carrying around some unresolved issues regarding his relationship with me, the nurse encouraged my father to (finally) talk with me about some of the things he apparently wanted to get off his chest.

My father was incredibly stubborn, so I can only imagine how difficult it was to persuade him to attempt to have a conversation with me about his feelings. Eventually, however, the nurse's efforts paid off (or so I was lead to believe). One day, approximately one week before my father died, the nurse informed me that my father wanted to speak with me. Sensing what this was about, I prepared myself for just about anything. However, even I would never have predicted how our strange and incredibly brief our conversation would be.

I walked with the nurse into my father's room and we sat on opposite sides of the bed. I touched my father's hand and let him know that I was there as he requested. My father acknowledged me and then turned to the nurse and said, "I want to tell my son that I'm proud of him."[20] That was it. That was all he could manage. After this meager utterance, my father simply looked straight ahead and closed his eyes as if to signal that the conversation was over. He never looked in my direction or did anything to suggest that he desired any input from me. The encounter was absolutely as weird as it undoubtedly sounds.

At the conclusion of *What Happened to You?*, Oprah describes her fractured relationship with her mother and their interactions at the end of her mother's life. It's a very moving passage and illustrates humanity at its best and most forgiving. Perhaps some of you are asking yourself why I didn't extend to my father some grace and help him express what he

---

[20] Never in his life did my father tell me that he was proud of me. I like to think he was proud of me, but he simply could never bring himself to communicate that to me.

apparently wanted (and perhaps needed) to express before he passed. The short answer is because I actively chose not to.

The writer John Mark Green has observed that "in a relationship, no amount of extra effort on your part can make up for a lack of effort on theirs." Once I sensed that my father wanted to make amends with me, as it were, before he died, I gave considerable thought to how I would respond to any such conversation between us. I didn't really want to have this sort of conversation with my father. I had long ago come to terms with my father's narcissism and parental shortcomings and had become content with the shape our relationship had taken. We were much less father and son and more like acquaintances with certain shared experiences. It was cordial but superficial. I had no interest in picking at that scar.

Thus, I concluded that if my father wanted me to help salve *his* soul, he would have to earn my participation. I didn't expect much from him in this regard because I knew he wasn't capable of much. I didn't expect him to meet me half-way or even one-quarter of the way. I simply wanted him to make the first step and say something *to me* that reflected some understanding that he knew that he failed me as a parent and that such was a large part of the reason we were not close. If he could simply exhibit even the slightest degree of self-awareness and self-reflection, I was willing to engage and help get him over the finish line, as it were. Even this was too much to ask of my father, however.

I feel like I haven't done my best work
yet.

Liza Minnelli

While my quest to become better at life and more
comfortable with myself continues, this seems like
an appropriate place to end this work. Having
reached this point, however, I find myself asking
several questions: "where am I?", "was writing this
book worth the effort?", and "do I really want to
share this work publicly?". Let's examine these in
reverse order.

I have no illusions that this work is particularly
noteworthy or will be read by that many people.
Nevertheless, I am confident that somebody (and
maybe even multiple somebodies) will benefit in
some way from reading this. Perhaps you know
somebody who is struggling with some of life's
inevitable garbage, in which case I'm confident there
is something in these pages that will enable you to
help them. Maybe you're simply intrigued by one or
more of the topics addressed herein. If so, reading
one or more of the books referenced herein may
enhance your knowledge and understanding of
something which impacts all of us far more than we
realize. Then, there is perhaps the most obvious (at
least to me) category of person that can potentially
benefit from this book. As I noted in the
Introduction, there is nothing unique about what
I've experienced. Thus, the likelihood that
somebody reading this has experienced, and failed to

adequately come to terms with, some trauma or garbage they experienced is, unfortunately, incredibly high. If this describes you, this work hopefully provides you some measure of motivation and encouragement to seek relief and begin to heal.

Finally, it may sound trite, but I do believe there is a benefit from talking about this stuff openly and honestly. Remaining silent and pretending that truly awful things don't happen to ourselves or others only diminishes our own emotional well-being. To put it a bit differently, maybe reading about a crazy old man airing his dirty (and very embarrassing) laundry for the world to see gives you the confidence or motivation to tackle what's eating you. And as previously noted, you don't even have to talk with a therapist or other professional. Just find somebody that provides you with an environment in which you can begin to regain your footing and toss aside some of the garbage weighing you down. So, yes, as embarrassed and uncomfortable as I am about sharing my experiences, I'm more than happy to share this work with anybody who wants to read it or share it with others.

As for whether writing this book was worth the effort, the answer is certainly "yes." As I alluded to in the Introduction, writing this book arose from my therapist's efforts to teach me how to modify the way my brain interprets and interacts with certain memories and events. In hindsight, I feel as if this effort has been fruitful. My work is certainly not complete, but no longer am I regularly assaulted by the remnants of certain events. This is not to suggest that I have forgotten the events and feelings in question. Contrary to what I was (unsuccessfully) attempting to do for far too many years, however, forgetting these things should never have been the goal. What I have come to understand is that with respect to these sorts of traumatic or assaultive memories, the goal is not to forget (which simply isn't possible) but to integrate.

As Dr. McDonald observes, "our brains process different events in different ways." Routine (i.e., non-threatening) events and occurrences get "encoded and filed away" in a manner that facilitates conscious retrieval and interaction. However, when you experience "something overwhelming. . .the recording mechanisms in your brain go a little haywire, and as a result, the [memory] is created, but is disorganized." This "atypical organization is by design," however. As McDonald explains:

> There's a somewhat inconvenient upshot of the efficient operation of the threat system: one of the things that gets slowed down is the recording mechanism in your brain. . .If a [memory] isn't recorded and filed, the trauma memory will stay in the present and manifest itself in symptoms.

> When your recording mechanism isn't fully online, instead of a coherent memory file, you get fragments –

sounds, colors, smells, phrases, tastes –
that are filed away in disorganized
ways. Just because they are
disorganized does not mean that they
don't get stored. In fact, they get
imprinted deeply. Your brain will hold
on to those things at all costs, because
again, they represent threat or danger,
and we learn our most vivid lessons
from fear.

As a result, these "memory fragments" are "not
organized and neatly filed away like the rest of your
memories." Rather, "they're just sort of thrown into
a cabinet" and "you relive them every time a
reminder pushes one of them to the surface." This
experience is as unenjoyable as it sounds which is
why many, myself included, fruitlessly and
counterproductively try and forget these memories
or experiences. Unfortunately, our brains just don't
work that way. Instead, what I am learning is that
the goal should instead be to integrate these
unpleasant memories. In a sense, take the
disorganized memory fragments that are causing so
much distress and organize them and file them in
your memory just like the hundreds of thousands of
other ordinary memories you have stored in your
brain.

One way to accomplish this is to transform these
memory fragments into a coherent story or
narrative. As Dr. McDonald explains:

When we render a traumatic event into story form, it starts to look like the rest of our memories. Memories that are organized in this way are recognizable as events from the past [rather than present dangers]. When we retell the events, the memory fragments our brain had hastily stuffed into its filing system in a haphazard, disorganized way become organized into a coherent memory. We pick up the scattered pieces like papers that had been dropped on the floor, put them in coherent order and right side up, and straighten the edges of the pile. Our brain can now file the whole memory neatly alongside other coherent memories from innocuous everyday events. We can engage with these memories and their content [like any other memory of non-threatening events]. We recognize it as an event from the past, and so we stop needing to relive it. Rather than continuing to be shot into the past, we begin to be able to navigate [the memory] with some control.

This process is much more complicated (and more difficult) than simply writing about vexing memories and events, however, writing about these things can certainly be part of this process. Thus, as I stated in the Introduction, I *had* to write this book and it has been a process from which I have benefitted greatly.

This brings us to the final question – where am I? or, probably more appropriately, how am I? Fortunately, the answer I can offer now, at the conclusion of this effort, is quite different from the answer I would have given when this work began. I'm feel like I'm doing pretty well at the moment, able, at long last, to move beyond a shadow that has seemingly engulfed me for far too long.

I'm at the conclusion of a meaningful career in public service. I'm heading into retirement feeling a tremendous sense of gratitude. I'm thankful for the life Lisa and I have created for ourselves. The friendships and connections I have developed over the years, which have helped me reach this point in life, will hopefully continue long into the future. While it has been difficult at times not to harbor truly corrosive levels of anger and regret, I have come to accept and embrace that I am where I am supposed to be and am living the life I'm supposed to live. Moreover, I believe I am, in certain ways, a better and stronger person because of what I have endured. As Oprah has observed, "there is no doubt that our strengths, vulnerabilities, and unique responses are an expression of what happened to us."

Still, there is much more work to do. Participating in therapy and writing this book has been incredibly beneficial. I have (hopefully) managed to get off my back for good a weight that has burdened me for many years. However, getting this weight off my back, while much welcomed, has brought into clearer focus other nettlesome problems. It's sort of like when a hurricane roars through an area. The immediate difficulty is getting the flood waters to recede, but it's only after that is accomplished that the true scope of the repair work is discernable.

So, while writing this book and undertaking the work which underlies it has been difficult and occupied much time and energy, it is in a sense only now that the real work begins. The challenges while several are not insurmountable. I'll save the details for my next book but with the continued support and encouragement of a great many people I'm confident that my efforts will bear fruit.

The End

www.ingramcontent.com/pod-product-compliance
Lightning Source LLC
Chambersburg PA
CBHW041719090426
42739CB00019B/3484